Table of Contents

Phonics

Table of Contents

Reading Comprehension

Grammar and Writing

Table of Contents

Color the Letter Partners

Letter partners are capital and small letters that go together. These pairs of letters are letter partners: **Aa, Bb, Cc, Dd, Ee, Ff, Gg, Hh, Ii, Jj, Kk, Ll, Mm, Nn, Oo, Pp, Qq, Rr, Ss, Tt, Uu, Vv, Ww, Xx, Yy, Zz.**

◆ **Directions:** Use a different color to color each pair of letter partners.

Letter Recognition

6

Partner Match

♦ **Directions:** Draw a line from each letter in the beehive to its partner letter.

7

Letter Recognition

Partner Search

♦ **Directions:** Color fish with letter partners yellow. Color the other fish blue. Follow the yellow path to the island.

Name

8

Sounds the Same

Different words may begin with the same sound.

Example: **Box** and **boy** begin with the same sound.
Cat and **dog** do not.

◆ **Directions:** Say each picture's name. Color the pictures in the box if their names begin with the same sound.

Auditory Discrimination

Tic-Tac-Toe

Name _____

♦ **Directions:** Find the three pictures in each game whose names begin with the same sound. Draw a line through them.

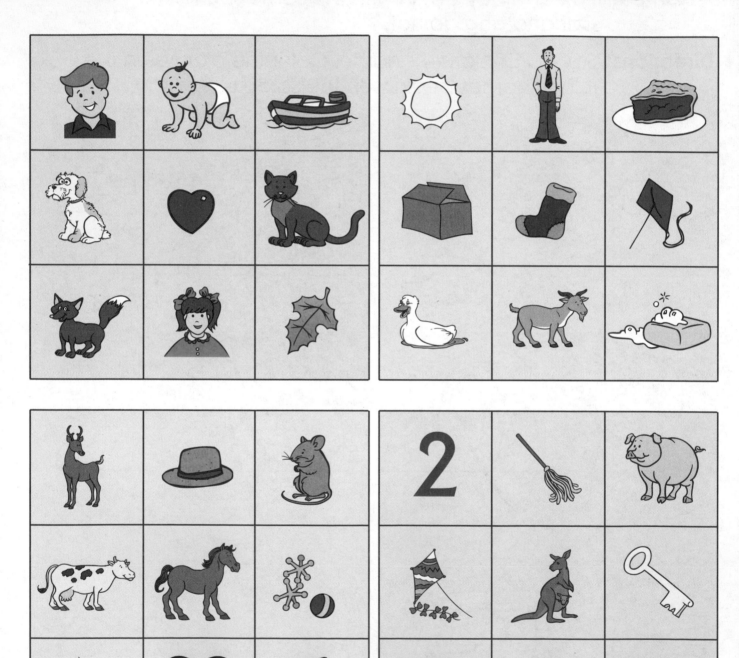

Read and Rhyme

Words that end with the same sounds are words that rhyme.

Hot and **pot** rhyme.
Hot and **pup** do not rhyme.

♦ **Directions:** Cut out the pictures at the bottom of the page. Say the name of each picture. In each row, glue the pictures whose names rhyme.

Auditory Discrimination

Write and Hear Mm

Name _____

M and **m** are letter partners.

Map begins with the sound of **Mm**.

♦ **Directions:** Trace the letter. Write it on the line.

M

m

♦ **Directions:** Color the pictures whose names begin with the sound of **m**.

Initial Consonant Mm

Write and Hear Ss

S and **s** are letter partners.

Sock begins with the sound of **Ss**.

♦ **Directions:** Trace the letter. Write it on the line.

S

s

♦ **Directions:** Circle the socks with pictures whose names begin with the sound of **s**.

Initial Consonant Ss

14

Write and Hear Tt

T and **t** are letter partners.

Tiger begins with the sound of **Tt**.

♦ **Directions:** Trace the letter. Write it on the line.

T

t

♦ **Directions:** Color the pictures whose names begin with the sound of **t**.

15

Initial Consonant Tt

Write and Hear Hh

Name

H and **h** are letter partners.

Hat begins with the sound of **Hh**.

♦ **Directions:** Trace the letter. Write it on the line.

H

h

♦ **Directions:** Play Tic-Tac-Toe. Find three pictures in a row whose names begin with the sound of **h**. Draw a line through them.

Initial Consonant Hh

16

Write and Hear Kk

Name _____

K and **k** are letter partners.

Kitten begins with the sound of **Kk**.

♦ **Directions:** Trace the letter. Write it on the line.

K -

k -

♦ **Directions:** Color the pictures whose names begin with the sound of **k**.

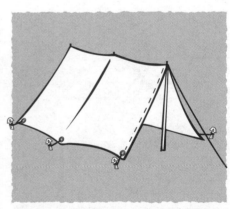

17

Initial Consonant Kk

Write and Hear Bb

Name

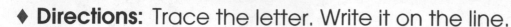

B and **b** are letter partners.

Ball begins with the sound of **Bb**.

♦ **Directions:** Trace the letter. Write it on the line.

B

b

♦ **Directions:** Color the bow if the name of the picture on the box begins with the sound of **b**.

Initial Consonant Bb

Write and Hear Ff

F and **f** are letter partners.

Fox begins with the sound of **Ff**.

◆ **Directions:** Trace the letter. Write it on the line.

F

f

◆ **Directions:** Help the farmer find the fox. Draw a line through the pictures whose names begin with the sound of **f**.

19

Initial Consonant Ff

Write and Hear Gg

G and **g** are letter partners.

Goat begins with the sound of **Gg**.

♦ **Directions:** Trace the letter. Write it on the line.

G -

g -

♦ **Directions:** Write **g** if the name of the picture begins with the sound of **g**.

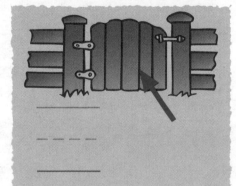

Initial Consonant Gg

20

Write and Hear Ll

L and **l** are letter partners.

Leaf begins with the sound of **Ll**.

♦ **Directions:** Trace the letter. Write it on the line.

L

l

♦ **Directions:** Color the leaves with pictures whose names begin with the sound of **l**.

21

Initial Consonant Ll

Write and Hear Nn

N and **n** are letter partners.

Nest begins with the sound of **Nn**.

♦ **Directions:** Trace the letter. Write it on the line.

N

n

♦ **Directions:** Color those pictures whose names begin with the sound of **n**.

Initial Consonant Nn

22

Write and Hear Dd

D and **d** are letter partners.

Desk begins with the sound of **Dd**.

♦ **Directions:** Trace the letter. Write it on the line.

D -

d -

♦ **Directions:** Color the pictures whose names begin with the sound of **d**.

Initial Consonant Dd

Write and Hear Ww

Name

W and **w** are letter partners.

Window begins with the sound of **Ww**.

♦ **Directions:** Trace the letter. Write it on the line.

W

w

♦ **Directions:** Color the curtains if the name of the picture begins with the sound of **w**.

Initial Consonant Ww

24

Write and Hear Cc

C and **c** are letter partners.

Cap begins with the sound of **Cc**.

♦ **Directions:** Trace the letter. Write it on the line.

C

c

♦ **Directions:** Play Tic-Tac-Toe. Find three pictures in a row whose names begin with the sound of **c**. Draw a line through them.

 25

Initial Consonant Cc

J and **j** are letter partners.

Jacket begins with the sound of **Jj**.

♦ **Directions:** Trace the letter. Write it on the line.

J

j

♦ **Directions:** Color the jack-in-the-box if the name of its picture begins with the sound of **j**.

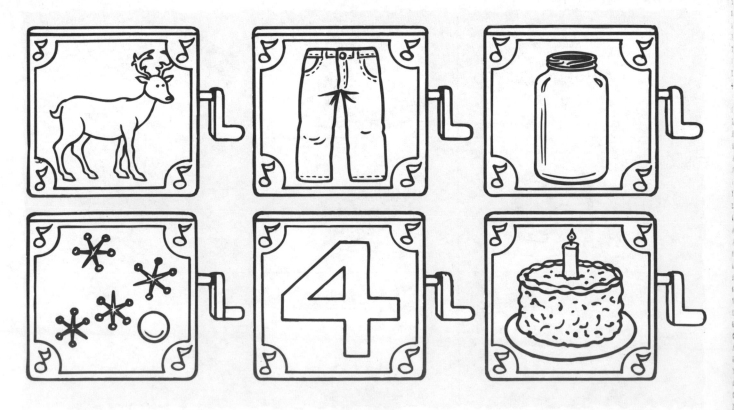

Write and Hear Rr

R and **r** are letter partners.

Ring begins with the sound of **Rr**.

♦ **Directions:** Trace the letter. Write it on the line.

R ————————————————————————

r ————————————————————————

♦ **Directions:** Write **r** on the line if the name of the picture begins with the sound of **r**.

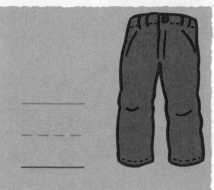

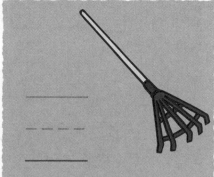

Initial Consonant Rr

Write and Hear Pp

P and **p** are letter partners.

Pen begins with the sound of **Pp**.

♦ **Directions:** Trace the letter. Write it on the line.

P

p

♦ **Directions:** Color the pictures whose names begin with the sound of **p**.

Initial Consonant Pp

28

Write and Hear Vv

Name _____

V and **v** are letter partners.

Vase begins with the sound of **Vv**.

♦ **Directions:** Trace the letter. Write it on the line.

V

v

♦ **Directions:** Trace the vases with pictures whose names begin with the sound of **v**. Use a crayon.

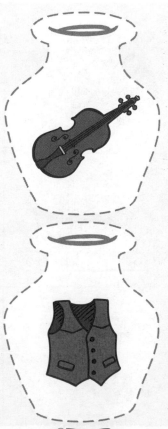

Initial Consonant Vv

Write and Hear Yy

Y and **y** are letter partners.

Yellow begins with the sound of **Yy**.

♦ **Directions:** Trace the letter. Write it on the line.

Y

y

♦ **Directions:** Play Tic-Tac-Toe. Find three pictures in a row whose names begin with the sound of **y**. Draw a line through them.

Initial Consonant Yy

30

Write and Hear Zz

Z and **z** are letter partners.

Zero begins with the sound of **Zz**.

♦ **Directions:** Trace the letter. Write it on the line.

Z

Z

♦ **Directions:** Help the zebra find the zoo. Connect all the pictures whose names begin with the sound of **z** from the zebra to the zoo.

31

Initial Consonant **Zz**

Write and Hear Qq

Q and **q** are letter partners.

Queen begins with the sound of **Qq**.

♦ **Directions:** Trace the letter. Write it on the line.

Q

q

♦ **Directions:** Write **q** on the line if the name in the picture begins with
the sound of **q**.

Initial Consonant Qq

32

Match Letters and Sounds

Name

◆ **Directions:** Cut out each letter at the bottom of the page. Find the picture whose name begins with the sound of that letter. Glue the letter in the box beside the picture.

Initial Consonants

Write and Hear Xx

X and **x** are letter partners.

Box ends with the sound of **Xx**.

box

♦ **Directions:** Trace the letter. Write it on the line.

X

X

♦ **Directions:** Look at the letter at the end of the row. Then, color the pictures whose names end with the sound of that letter. Circle the pictures whose names end with **x**.

Final Consonants

How Does It End?

◆ Directions: Write a letter from the box to complete each word.

m   k   b   n   p   r   l   d   g

dru_____

sta_____

be_____

tai_____

bi_____

lo_____

fa_____

mo_____

boo_____

Final Consonants

 36

Name _____

♦ **Directions:** Say the name of each picture. Listen to the sound in the middle of the word. Fill in the circle beside the letter that stands for that sound.

○ s
○ b
○ d

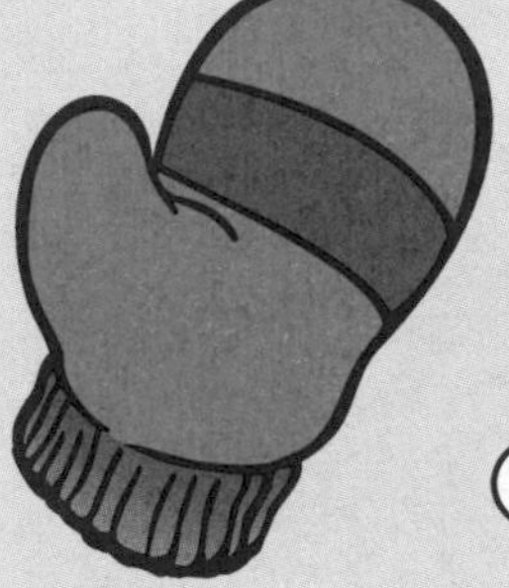

○ t
○ x
○ l

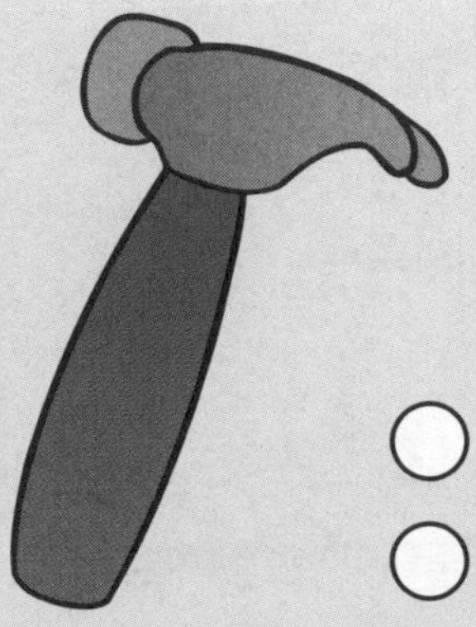

○ m
○ z
○ p

○ t
○ p
○ k

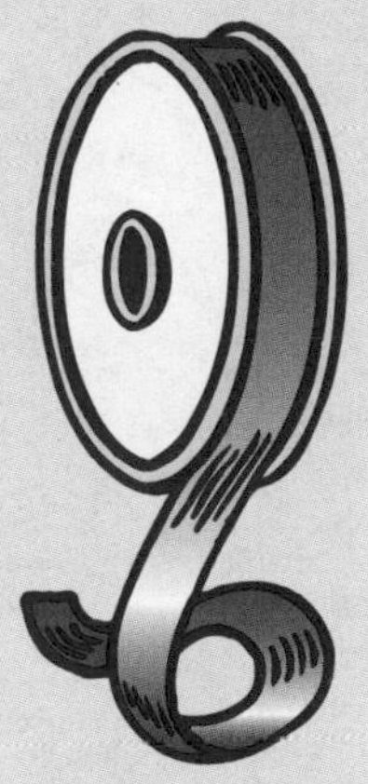

○ b
○ x
○ w

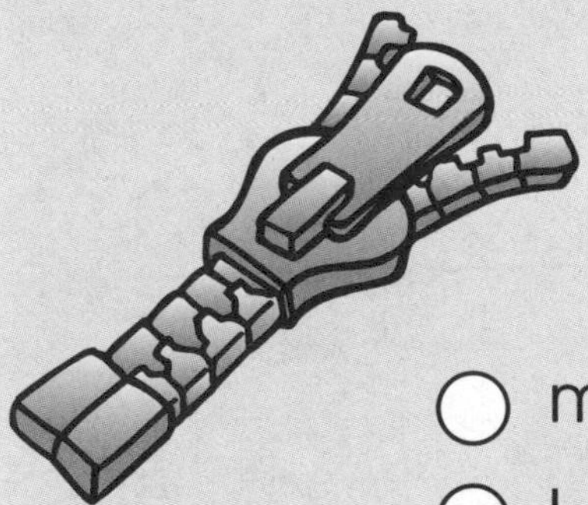

○ m
○ l
○ p

○ l
○ s
○ r

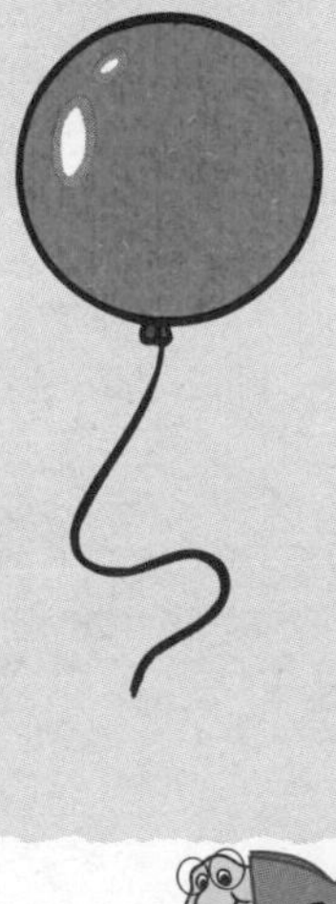

○ m
○ l
○ k

○ p
○ b
○ g

37

Middle Consonants

♦ **Directions:** Write the missing letters.

ro ___ ot   ti ___ er   ca ___ el

ba ___ y   se ___ en   sa ___ ad

po ___ y   dra ___ on   me ___ on

Name _____

◆ **Directions:** One letter is missing in each word. Write the missing letter on the line.

___og

bo___

un___

he___

tu___ip

___op

___to

___lea

wa___on

Consonants in All Positions

Consonant Review

◆ Directions: Write all the missing consonants.

_____ a

_____ o

_____ i

_____ e

_____ a

_____ a e

_____ oa

_____ a

_____ a

Meet Short a

Listen for the sound of short **a** in **van**.

♦ **Directions:** Trace the letter. Write it on the line.

 van

A

a

♦ **Directions:** Color the pictures whose names have the short **a** sound.

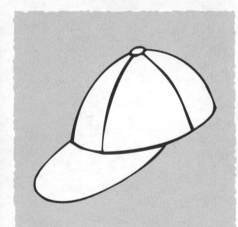

Short Vowel a

Short a Maze

♦ **Directions:** Help the cat get to the bag. Connect all the pictures whose names have the short **a** sound from the cat to the bag.

Short Vowel a

42

Short a Picture Match

♦ **Directions:** Cut out the cards. Read the words.
Match the words and the pictures.

hat	van	bat	ham
bag	man	map	fan

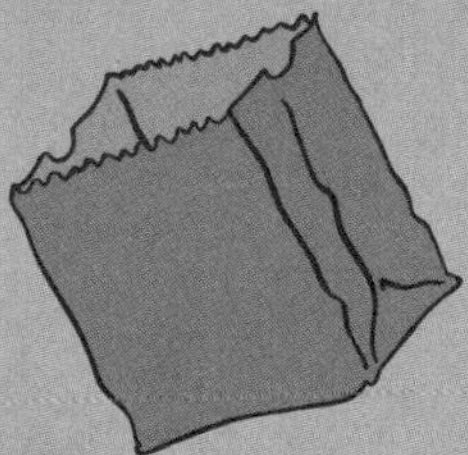

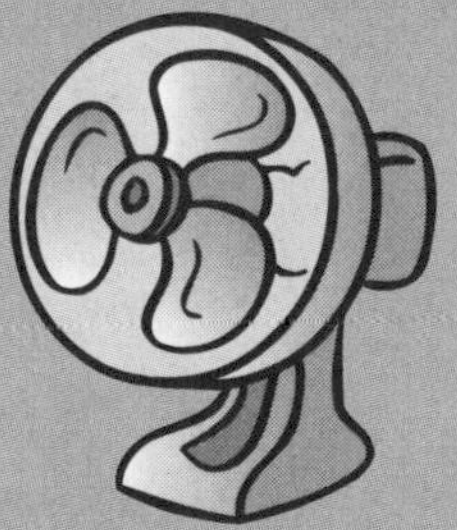

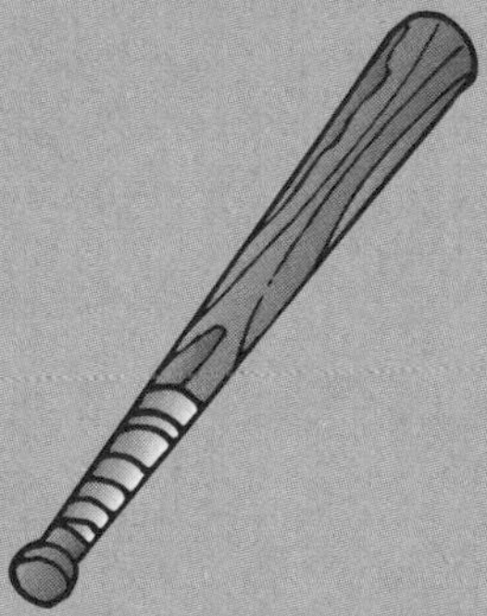

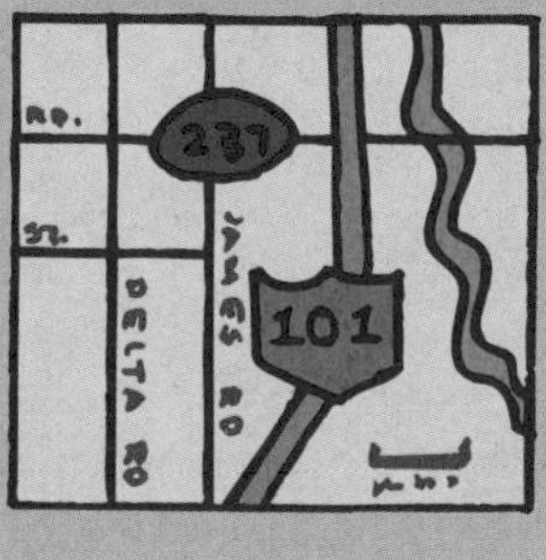

43

Short Vowel a

Meet Short i

Listen for the sound of short **i** in **pig**.

Name _____

pig

♦ **Directions:** Trace the letter. Write it on the line.

I

i

♦ **Directions:** Say the name of each picture. Color the trim on the bib if the name has the short **i** sound.

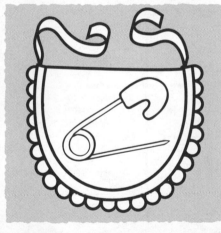 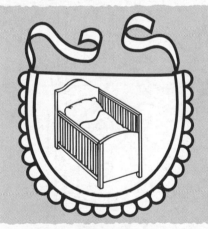 

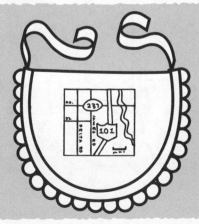  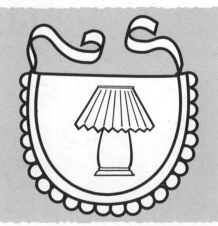

Short Vowel i

Read and Color Short i

♦ **Directions:** Say the name of each picture. Color the pictures whose names have the short **i** sound. The words in the box will give you hints.

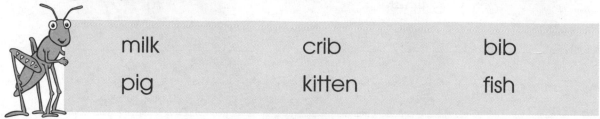

| milk | crib | bib |
| pig | kitten | fish |

Short Vowel i   46

The Donkey's Tail

◆ **Directions:** Find the donkey tails with pictures whose names have the short **i** sound. Cut them out. Glue those tails onto the donkeys.

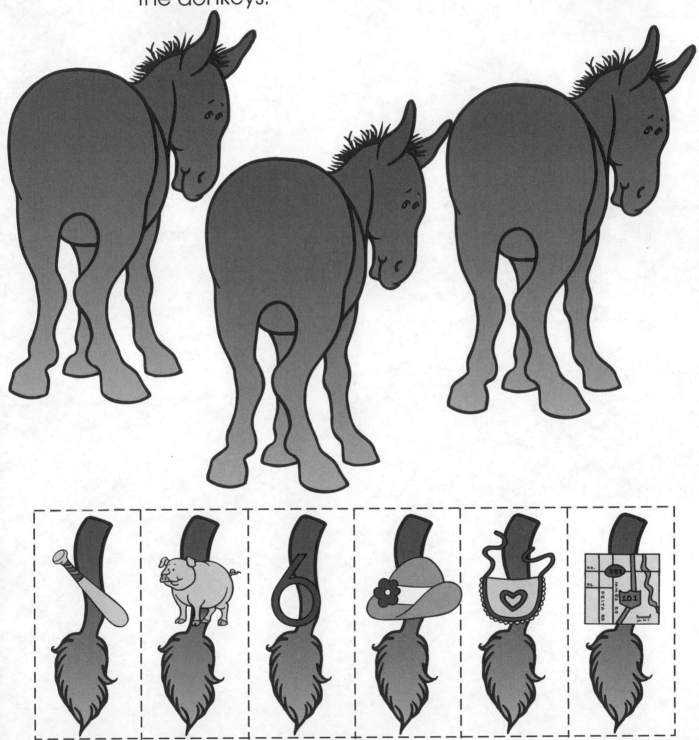

47

Short Vowel i

Meet Short u

Listen for the sound of short **u** in **bug**.

♦ **Directions:** Trace the letter.
Write it on the line.

bug

U _ _ _ _ _ _ _ _ _ _ _ _ _ _ _ _ _ _

u _ _ _ _ _ _ _ _ _ _ _ _ _ _ _ _ _ _

♦ **Directions:** Say the name of each picture. Color the sun yellow if
you hear the short **u** sound in the name.

Short Vowel u

Short u Tic-Tac-Toe

Name

♦ **Directions:** Color the pictures whose names have the short **u** sound. Then, play Tic-Tac-Toe. Draw a line through three colored pictures in a row.

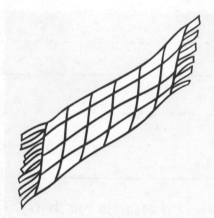

Short Vowel u

50

Feed the Pup

Name

♦ **Directions:** Cut out the picture cards. Say the name of each picture. If the name has the sound of short **u**, glue the card in the pup's bowl.

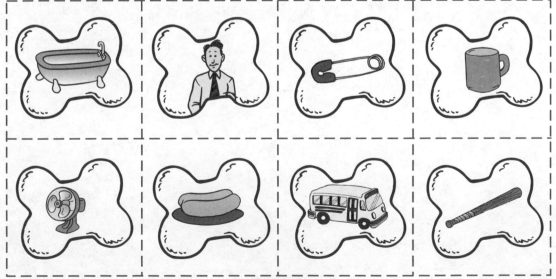

Short Vowel u

Meet Short o

Listen for the sound of short **o** in **fox**.

fox

♦ **Directions:** Trace the letter.
Write it on the line.

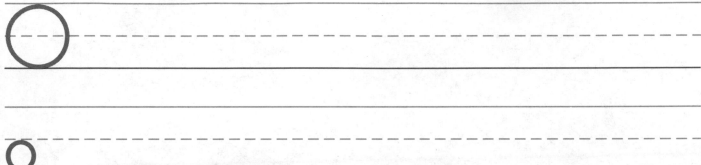

♦ **Directions:** Say the name of each picture. Write **o** under the picture
if the name has the short **o** sound.

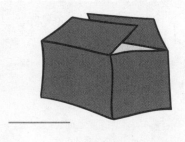

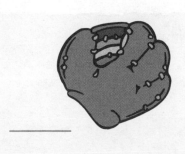

Short Vowel o

Find Short o Words

♦ **Directions:** Underline the pictures whose names have the short **o** sound.

♦ **Directions:** The words that match the underlined pictures above are hidden in this puzzle. Circle the words. They may go **across** or **down**.

```
I  T  L  J  B  Z

M  O  O  C  O  T

O  P  G  U  X  U

P  D  O  G  L  P
```

Short Vowel o   54

Short o Puzzles

♦ **Directions:** Cut out the puzzle pieces. Match each picture with its name.

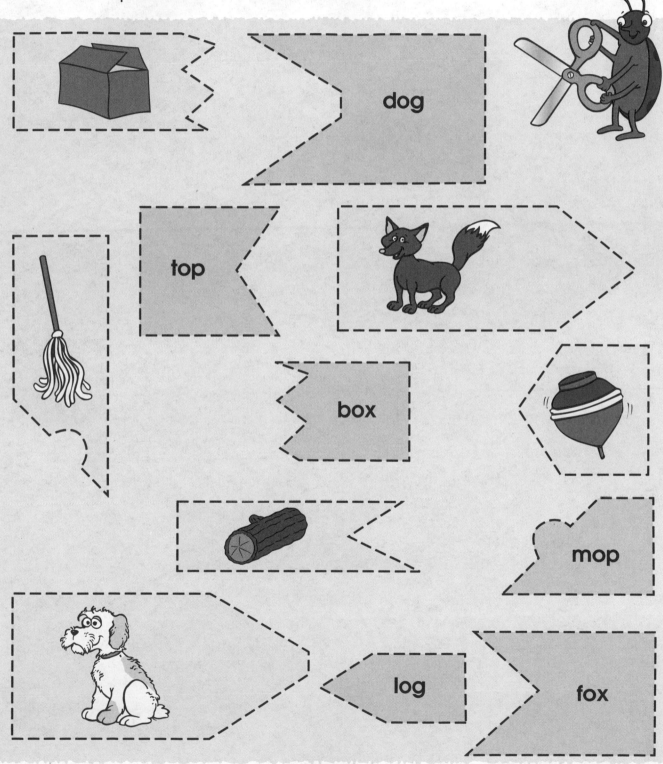

dog

top

box

mop

log

fox

Short Vowel o

Meet Short e

Name _____

Listen for the sound of short **e** in **hen**.

♦ **Directions:** Trace the letter.
Write it on the line.

hen

E

e

♦ **Directions:** Color the pictures whose names have the short **e** sound.

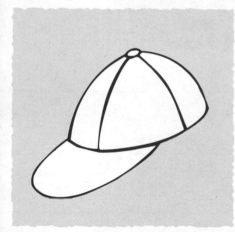

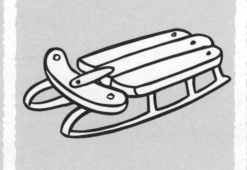

Short Vowel e

A Matching Game

Name

♦ **Directions:** Draw a line to connect each picture with its matching short **e** word.

men

jet

hen

web

ten

bed

Short Vowel Scrapbook

Name _____

A Cut and Fold Book

♦ **Directions:** The pages of your Cut and Fold Book are on the back of this sheet. First, follow the directions below to make the book. Then, follow the directions on the small pages of your Cut and Fold Book. Show your *Short Vowel Scrapbook* to a family member or friend. Think of other words you could draw for each short vowel sound.

1. Tear the page out of the book.

2. Fold page along Line A so that the top meets the bottom. Make sure Line A is on the outside of the fold.

3. Fold along Line B to make the book.

59

Short Vowel Review

Draw a picture of something
whose name has the short **o**
sound.

Draw a picture of something
whose name has the short **u**
sound.

Draw a picture of something
whose name has the short **i**
sound.

Line B

Line A

Draw a picture of something
whose name has the short **e**
sound.

Draw a picture of something
whose name has the short **a**
sound.

Finish-the-Word Puzzles

Name

♦ **Directions:** Write a vowel in the middle of each puzzle that will make a word across and down.

	w	
p		t
	b	

	m	
d		g
	p	

	f	
m		p
	n	

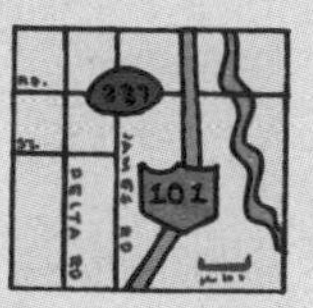

	w	
p		g
	n	

	h	
b		x
	t	

	b	
s		n
	s	

Short Vowel Review

Name the Short Vowel

Name _____

♦ **Directions:** Say the name of the picture. Listen for the short vowel sound. Then, fill in the correct circle.

○ short **a** ○ short **e** ○ short **i** ○ short **o** ○ short **u**		○ short **a** ○ short **e** ○ short **i** ○ short **o** ○ short **u**		○ short **a** ○ short **e** ○ short **i** ○ short **o** ○ short **u**
○ short **a** ○ short **e** ○ short **i** ○ short **o** ○ short **u**		○ short **a** ○ short **e** ○ short **i** ○ short **o** ○ short **u**		○ short **a** ○ short **e** ○ short **i** ○ short **o** ○ short **u**
○ short **a** ○ short **e** ○ short **i** ○ short **o** ○ short **u**		○ short **a** ○ short **e** ○ short **i** ○ short **o** ○ short **u**		○ short **a** ○ short **e** ○ short **i** ○ short **o** ○ short **u**

Short Vowel Review

62

Meet Long a

Name

 cake

Listen for the sound of long **a** in **cake**.

♦ **Directions:** Color the pictures whose names have the long **a** sound.

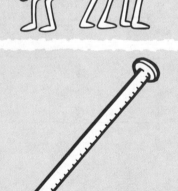

 63

Long Vowel a

Write Long a

The letters **a_e** usually stand for the long **a** sound.

lake

♦ **Directions:** Write the missing vowels.

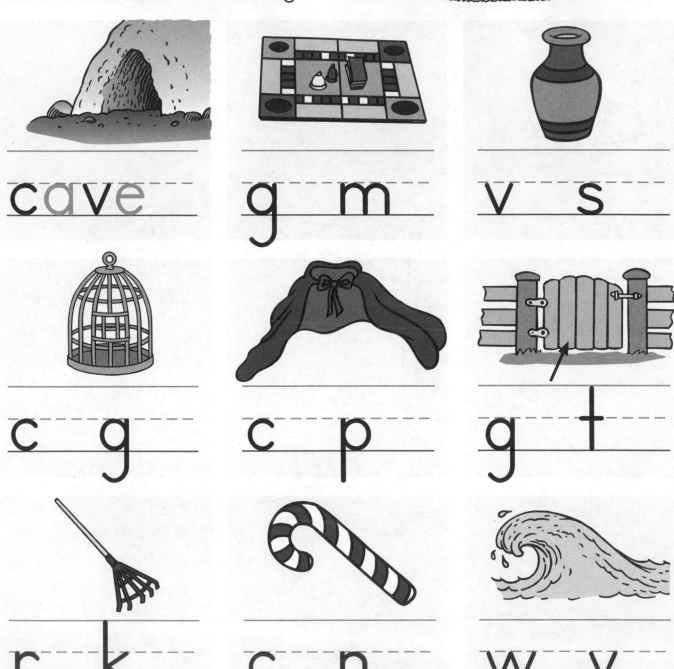

c a v e

g ___ m

v ___ s

c ___ g

c ___ p

g ___ t

r ___ k

c ___ n

w ___ v

Long Vowel a

64

Meet Long i

Listen for the sound of long **i** in **bike**.
Look for **i__e**.

bik**e**

♦ **Directions:** Fill in the circle beside the name of the picture.

○ dim
○ date
○ dime

○ five
○ fix
○ fame

○ kite
○ cat
○ kit

○ pane
○ pin
○ pine

○ tin
○ tire
○ tale

○ red
○ ride
○ rid

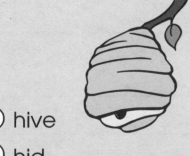

○ hive
○ hid
○ had

○ nip
○ name
○ nine

○ fame
○ fire
○ fin

Long Vowel i

Long i and Short i

Name _____

♦ **Directions:** Write the name of the picture on the correct line.

bike

pig

bib

dime

six

pine

five

pin

Long Vowel i

_____

- - - - - - - - - - -

_____

- - - - - - - - - - -

_____

- - - - - - - - - - -

_____

- - - - - - - - - - -

_____

Short Vowel i

_____

- - - - - - - - - - -

_____

- - - - - - - - - - -

_____

- - - - - - - - - - -

_____

- - - - - - - - - - -

_____

Long Vowel i

Meet Long u

Name

Listen for the sound of long **u** in **mule**. The letters **u_e** and **ue** usually stand for the long **u** sound.

mule

♦ **Directions:** Circle the pictures whose names have the long **u** sound.

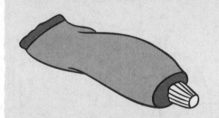

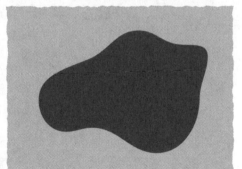

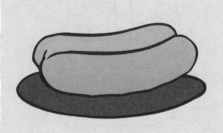

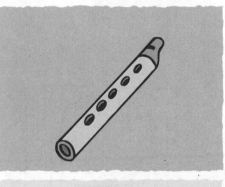

June				
	1	2	3	4	5
6	7	8	9	10	11	12
13	14	15	16	17	18	19
20	21	22	23	24	25	26
27	28	28	30			

Long Vowel u

♦ **Directions:** Each word in the box has the sound of long **u**. Color the picture that matches each word in the box.

mule	glue	cubes	flute

Meet Long o

Name _____

Listen for the sound of long **o** in **rose**.

rose

♦ **Directions:** Say the name of each picture. Decide whether the vowel sound you hear is long **o** or short **o**. Fill in the circle beside long **o** or short **o**.

○ Long o   ○ Short o

○ Long o   ○ Short o

○ Long o   ○ Short o

○ Long o   ○ Short o

○ Long o   ○ Short o

○ Long o   ○ Short o

○ Long o   ○ Short o

○ Long o   ○ Short o

○ Long o   ○ Short o

○ Long o   ○ Short o

○ Long o   ○ Short o

○ Long o   ○ Short o

Long Vowel o

Circle and Write

Name _____

The letters **o_e** and **oe** usually stand for the long **o** sound.

h**ose**

♦ **Directions:** Circle the name of each picture. Then, write the name on the line.

rob
rib
robe

_____
_ _ _ _ _ _ _ _ _
_____

not
note
net

_____
_ _ _ _ _ _ _ _ _
_____

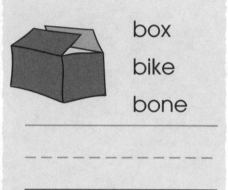

box
bike
bone

_____
_ _ _ _ _ _ _ _ _
_____

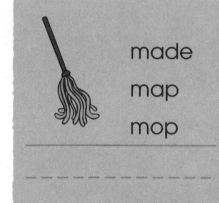

made
map
mop

_____
_ _ _ _ _ _ _ _ _
_____

cone
cane
can

_____
_ _ _ _ _ _ _ _ _
_____

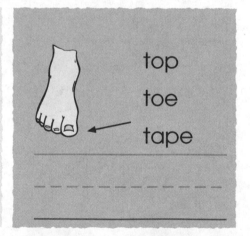

top
toe
tape

_____
_ _ _ _ _ _ _ _ _
_____

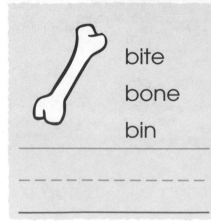

bite
bone
bin

_____
_ _ _ _ _ _ _ _ _
_____

date
dig
dog

_____
_ _ _ _ _ _ _ _ _
_____

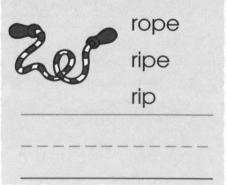

rope
ripe
rip

_____
_ _ _ _ _ _ _ _ _
_____

Meet Long e

Listen for the sound of long **e** in **bee**. The letters **ee** and **ea** usually stand for the long **e** sound.

b**ee**

♦ **Directions:** Write the name of the picture on the correct line.

 seal

 ten

 beet

 jeep

leaf

 bed

 red

 seat

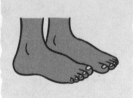 feet

ee	ea	Short Vowel e

Long Vowel e

Long Vowel Crossword

♦ **Directions:** Fill in the puzzle with the correct words.

Across

1.

4.

5.

Down

1.

2.

3.

Long Vowel Review

Long Vowel Puzzles

Name

♦ **Directions:** Cut out the puzzle pieces. Match each picture with its name.

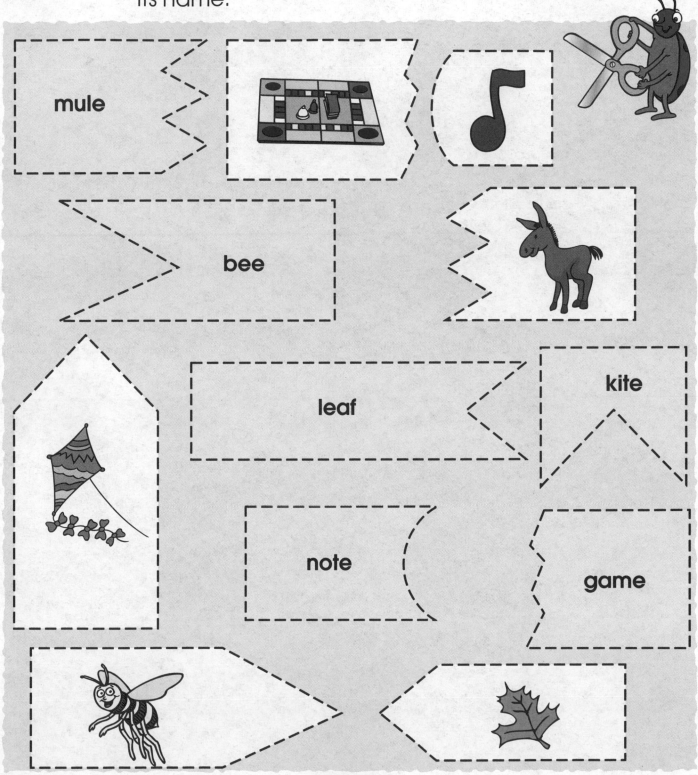

73

Long Vowel Review

The Sounds of y

A **y** at the end of a word can have the long **i** sound or the long **e** sound. Listen for the long **i** sound in **fly**. Listen for the long **e** sound in **pony**.

fly    pony

◆ **Directions:** Say the name of each picture. Listen for the sound of **y** at the end of the word. Circle either long **i** or long **e**.

sky

Long i   Long e

baby

Long i   Long e

bunny

Long i   Long e

cry

Long i   Long e

penny

Long i   Long e

muddy

Long i   Long e

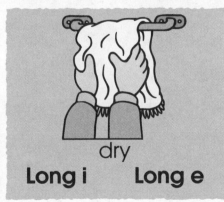

dry

Long i   Long e

twenty

Long i   Long e

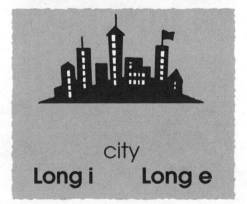

city

Long i   Long e

y as a Vowel

Which Sound of y?

Name

◆ **Directions:** Say the name of each picture. If the final **y** stands for the long **e** sound, color the picture green. If the **y** stands for the long **i** sound, color the picture yellow.

pony

fly

fifty

candy

dry

penny

cherry

sky

bunny

y as a Vowel

Sounds of c and g

Name

Consonants **c** and **g** each have two sounds. Listen for the soft **c** sound in **pencil**. Listen for the hard **c** sound in **cup**.

Listen for the soft **g** sound in **giant**. Listen for the hard **g** sound in **goat**. **C** and **g** usually have the soft sound when they are followed by **e**, **i** or **y**.

♦ **Directions:** Say the name of each picture. Listen for the sound of **c** or **g**. Then, read the words in each list. Circle the words that have that sound of **c** or **g**.

Hard c   cup

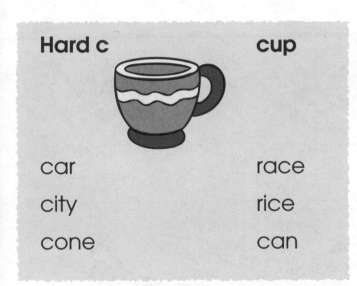

car   race

city   rice

cone   can

Soft c   pencil

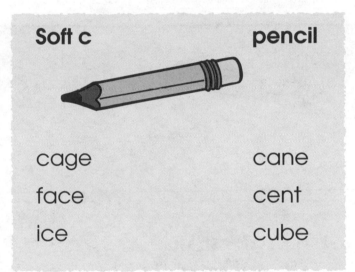

cage   cane

face   cent

ice   cube

Hard g   goat

good   magic

dragon   gum

stage   gentle

Soft g   giant

garden   gem

page   giraffe

gas   gorilla

Hard and Soft c and g

Hard and Soft c and g

Name _____

♦ **Directions:** Underline the letter that follows the **c** or **g** in each word.
Write **hard** if the word has the hard **c** or hard **g** sound.
Write **soft** if the word has the soft **c** or soft **g** sound.

car

_____
- - - - - - - - - - - -
_____

pencil

_____
- - - - - - - - - - - -
_____

giant

_____
- - - - - - - - - - - -
_____

gum

_____
- - - - - - - - - - - -
_____

wagon

_____
- - - - - - - - - - - -
_____

gym

_____
- - - - - - - - - - - -
_____

gem

_____
- - - - - - - - - - - -
_____

cymbals

_____
- - - - - - - - - - - -
_____

cup

_____
- - - - - - - - - - - -
_____

cot

_____
- - - - - - - - - - - -
_____

celery

_____
- - - - - - - - - - - -
_____

goat

_____
- - - - - - - - - - - -
_____

Hard and Soft c and g

78

Consonant Blends With r

Sometimes two consonants at the beginning of a word blend together. Listen for the **dr** blend in **dragon**. **Gr, fr, cr, tr, br** and **pr** are also **r** blends.

dr

dragon

♦ **Directions:** Draw a line from each consonant blend to the picture whose name begins with the same sound.

dr

br

cr

tr

pr

gr

fr

Initial Consonant Blends: r Blends

Fill the Tray

♦ **Directions:** Read the menu. Circle the words that have **r** blends. On the tray, draw pictures of the foods whose names you circled.

bread	pretzel	meat
butter	milk	grapes
salad	French fries	ice cream

80

Consonant Blends With l

Name _____

Listen for the **cl** blend in **clown**. **Gl**, **pl**, **fl** and **bl** are also **l** blends.

clown

♦ **Directions:** Look at the **l** blend at the beginning of each row. Color the picture whose name begins with that sound.

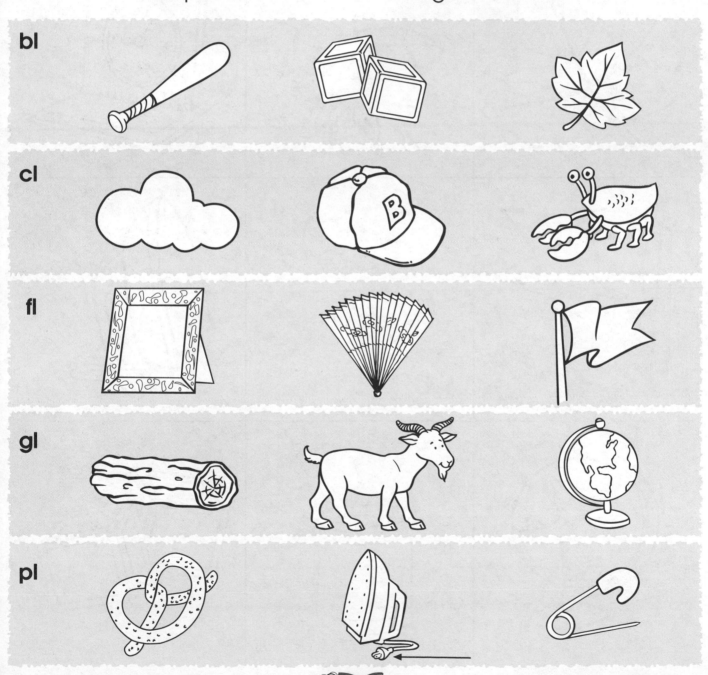

bl

cl

fl

gl

pl

81

Initial Consonant Blends: l Blends

L Blend Tic-Tac-Toe

Name

♦ **Directions:** Color the pictures whose names begin with **l** blends.
Draw a line through three colored pictures in a row to
score a Tic-Tac-Toe.

Consonant Blends With s

Name

Listen for the **sk** blend in **skunk**. **Sm**, **st**, **sp**, **sw**, **sc**, **squ**, **sl** and **sn** are also **s** blends.

skunk

♦ **Directions:** Say the name of each picture. Circle the **s** blend you hear at the beginning of the name.

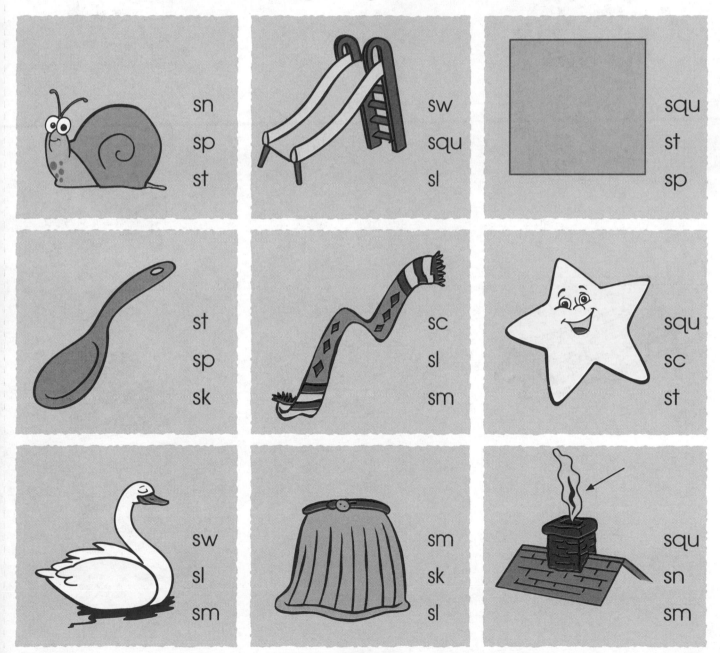

sn
sp
st

sw
squ
sl

squ
st
sp

st
sp
sk

sc
sl
sm

squ
sc
st

sw
sl
sm

sm
sk
sl

squ
sn
sm

Initial Consonant Blends: s Blends

Match Pictures and Blends

♦ **Directions:** Draw a line from each **s** blend to the picture whose name begins with that sound.

squ

sp

sw

sl

sk

sn

st

sm

Initial Consonant Blends: s Blends 　　84

Blends at the Ends

Some consonant blends come at the ends of words.
Listen for the **nd** blend at the end of the word **round**.
Mp, **ng**, **nt**, **sk**, **nk** and **st** can also be ending blends.

rou**nd**

♦ **Directions:** Say the name of each picture. Circle the blend you
hear at the end of the name.

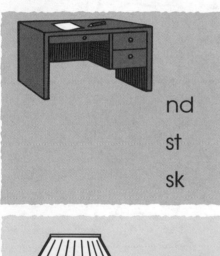   nd
st
sk

   nt
nk
ng

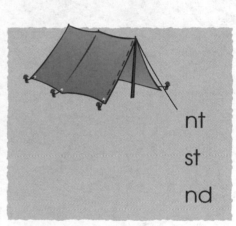   nt
st
nd

   nd
ng
mp

   ng
nt
nd

   nd
nk
st

   st
nt
nd

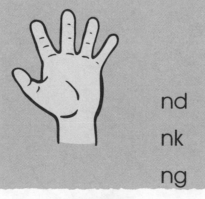   nd
nk
ng

   nt
sk
st

     Final Blends

Follow the Final Blends

Name

♦ **Directions:** Find the notes with pictures whose names end with consonant blends. Color them yellow. Draw a line through the yellow notes from the band to the tent.

Final Blends

86

Missing Blends

♦ **Directions:** Fill in the circle beside the missing blend in each word.

__ain	__an	te__
○ sk	○ sl	○ sk
○ tr	○ sm	○ nt
○ pr	○ sw	○ ng

__ate	__ate	__ide
○ sk	○ pl	○ sk
○ sm	○ pr	○ cl
○ cr	○ sp	○ sl

__ail	__ess	de__
○ ng	○ pr	○ st
○ sn	○ dr	○ nd
○ st	○ nd	○ sk

Consonant Blend Review

More Missing Blends

♦ **Directions:** Fill in the circle beside the missing blend in each word.

ri__	__y	__apes
○ nt	○ sl	○ gr
○ st	○ fl	○ cl
○ ng	○ pl	○ sk
__obe	ha__	__og
○ sl	○ nd	○ gr
○ gl	○ ng	○ tr
○ gr	○ sk	○ fr
__y	__ider	la__
○ sk	○ pr	○ st
○ sm	○ sl	○ mp
○ nt	○ sp	○ ng

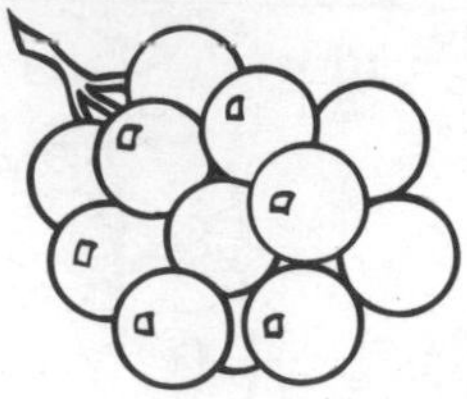

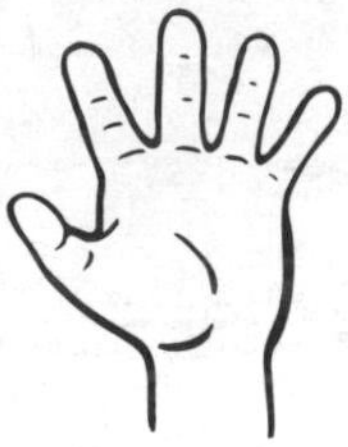

Consonant Blend Review

88

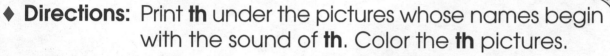

Consonant Digraph th

Some consonants work together to stand for a new sound. They are called **consonant digraphs**. Listen for the sound of consonant digraph **th** in **think**.

think

♦ **Directions:** Print **th** under the pictures whose names begin with the sound of **th**. Color the **th** pictures.

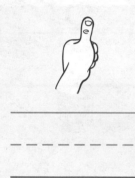

_____

- - - - - - - - - -

_____

_____

- - - - - - - - - -

_____

2

_____

- - - - - - - - - -

_____

_____

- - - - - - - - - -

_____

_____

- - - - - - - - - -

_____

_____

- - - - - - - - - -

_____

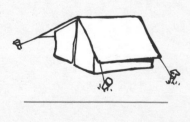

_____

- - - - - - - - - -

_____

_____

- - - - - - - - - -

_____

_____

- - - - - - - - - -

_____

Initial Digraph th

Think About th

Name _____

♦ **Directions:** Say the name of each picture. Fill in the missing letter or letters.

____ink   ____orn   ____orn

10
____en   ____umb   30
            ____irty

♦ **Directions:** Find and circle these **th** words in the puzzle. The words may go **across** or **down**.

| think | thorn | thumb | thirty |

```
T  T  H  I  R  T  Y
T  H  I  N  K  H  J
H  O  B  H  N  U  L
O  R  N  E  H  M  X
J  N  H  R  T  B  Y
```

Consonant Digraph sh

Listen for the sound of consonant digraph **sh** in **sheep**.

♦ **Directions:** Color the pictures whose names begin with the sound of **sh**.

sheep

Initial Digraph sh

Change a Word

♦ **Directions:** Make a new word by changing the beginning sound to **sh**. Write the new word on the line.

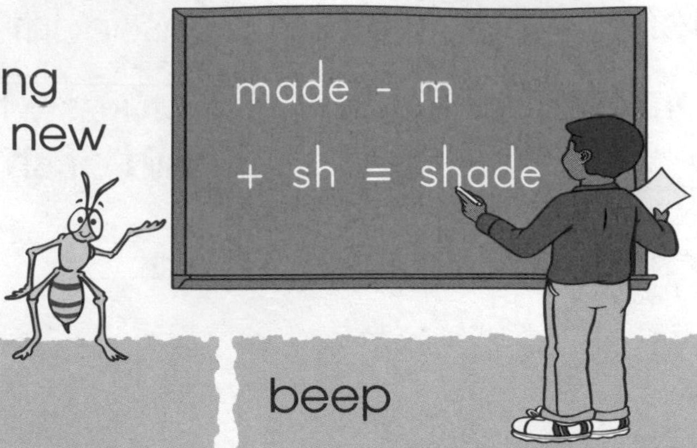

made – m
+ sh = shade

zip
_____
_____

sell
_____
_____

beep
_____
_____

tin
_____
_____

line
_____
_____

lift
_____
_____

red
_____
_____

cape
_____
_____

cave
_____
_____

top
_____
_____

bake
_____
_____

feet
_____
_____

Initial Digraph sh

92

Consonant Digraph wh

Name _____

◆ **Directions:** Write **wh**, **th** or **sh** to complete each word.

_____ eel

_____ ale

_____ eep

_____ ink

_____ eat

_____ orn

_____ ip

30

_____ irty

_____ ite

Initial Digraph wh

Wheel of Fortune

Name

Listen for the sound of consonant digraph **wh** in **whale**.

whale

♦ **Directions:** Color the pictures whose names begin with consonant digraph **wh**.

Initial Digraph wh

Consonant Digraph ch

Listen for the sound of consonant digraph **ch** in **cherry**.

cherry

♦ **Directions:** Trace the cherry if the name of the picture begins with the **ch** sound. Use a red crayon.

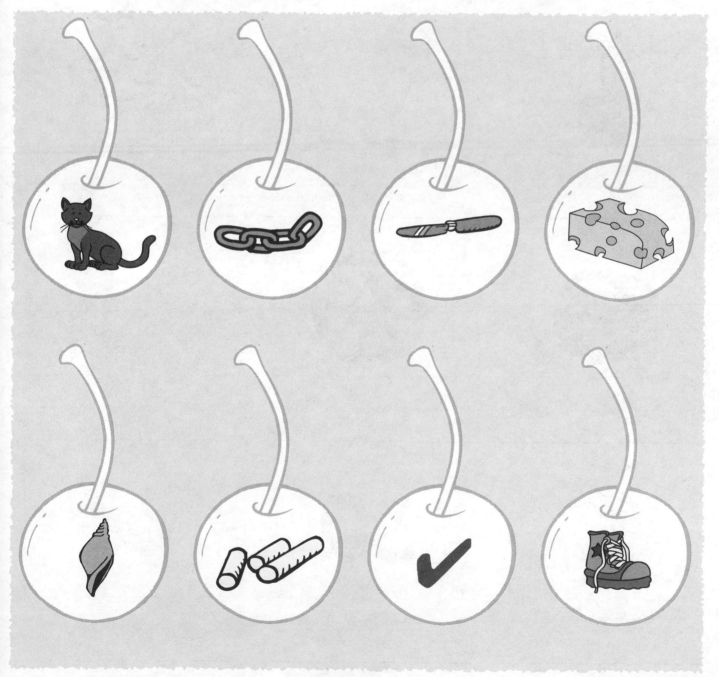

Initial Digraph ch

♦ **Directions:** Write a word from the box to label each picture.

chest	check	sheep
chimp	cherry	thirty
chain	cheese	wheel

_____

- - - - - - - -

_____

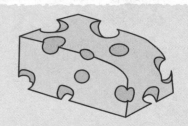

_____

- - - - - - - -

_____

30

_____

- - - - - - - -

_____

Consonant Digraph kn

Listen for the sound of consonant digraph
kn in **knot**. The **k** is silent.

knot

♦ **Directions:** Color the pictures whose names begin with the
kn sound. Connect all the colored pictures from
the knight to his horse.

Initial Digraph kn

Consonant Digraph wr

Listen for the sound of consonant digraph **wr** in **wren**.
The **w** is silent.

wren

♦ **Directions:** Write a word from the box to label each picture.
Color the pictures whose names begin with **wr**.

web	wrist	wring	wrap	
worm	write	wreath	wink	wrench

_____

___ ___ ___ ___ ___

_____

_____

___ ___ ___ ___ ___

_____

_____

___ ___ ___ ___ ___

_____

Initial Digraph wr

98

Ending Digraphs

Name _____

Some words end with consonant digraphs. Listen for the ending digraphs in **duck**, **moth**, **dish** and **branch**.

du**ck**   mo**th**   di**sh**    bran**ch**

♦ **Directions:** Say the name of each picture. Circle the letters that stand for the ending sound.

   ck th sh ch

   ck th sh wh

   ck th sh ch

   ck th sh ch

   ck th sh ch

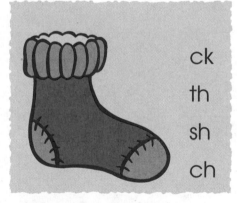   ck th sh ch

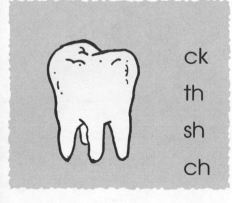   ck th sh ch

   ck th sh ch

   ck th sh ch

 99

Final Consonant Digraphs

Hear and Write Digraphs

◆ **Directions:** Write **ck**, **th**, **sh** or **ch** to complete each word.

_____

- - - - - - - - -

_____

_____

- - - - - - - - -

_____

_____

- - - - - - - - -

_____

_____

- - - - - - - - -

_____

_____

- - - - - - - - -

_____

_____

- - - - - - - - -

_____

_____

- - - - - - - - -

_____

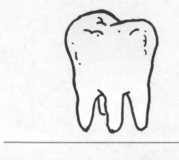

_____

- - - - - - - - -

_____

_____

- - - - - - - - -

_____

Final Consonant Digraphs

 100

Missing Digraphs

_____
Name

♦ **Directions:** Fill in the circle beside the missing digraph in each word.

__ale	pea__	__ife
○ wh	○ ck	○ kn
○ wr	○ th	○ ch
○ ch	○ ch	○ wr

__imp	__ell	clo__
○ ck	○ ch	○ ck
○ kn	○ sh	○ ch
○ ch	○ ck	○ kn

__ite	fi__	__orn
○ kn	○ ch	○ th
○ wr	○ sh	○ wr
○ th	○ th	○ ch

Consonant Digraph Review

Missing Digraphs

Name

♦ **Directions:** Fill in the circle beside the missing digraph in each word.

so___	___ain	___eath
○ ck	○ th	○ wr
○ ch	○ ch	○ wh
○ kn	○ sh	○ kn

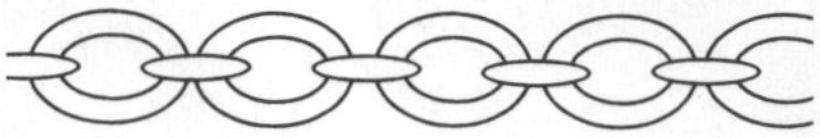

___ip	ben___	___eel
○ th	○ ck	○ sh
○ sh	○ th	○ th
○ ck	○ ch	○ wh

___ight	too___	___ench
○ kn	○ ch	○ kn
○ th	○ ck	○ wr
○ wr	○ th	○ th

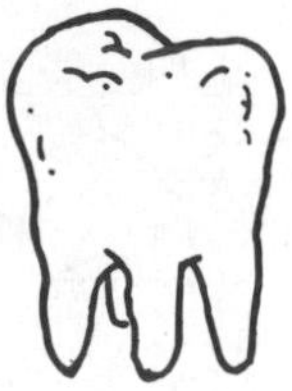

Consonant Digraph Review

Tricky ar

Name

When **r** follows a vowel, it changes the vowel's sound.
Listen for the **ar** sound in **star**.

st**ar**

♦ **Directions:** Color the pictures whose
names have the **ar** sound.

 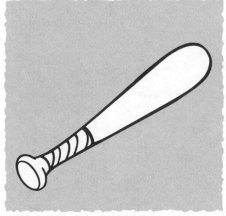 

 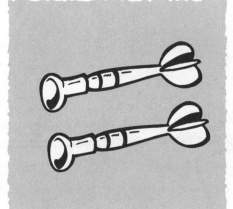 

 103

r-Controlled Vowels

Write ar or or

Listen for the **or** sound in **horn**.

horn

♦ **Directions:** Write **ar** or **or** to complete each word.

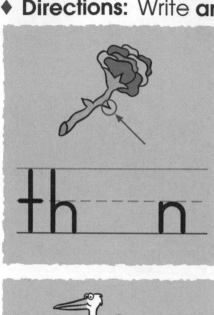

th___n

c___t

f___ty

st___k

c___n

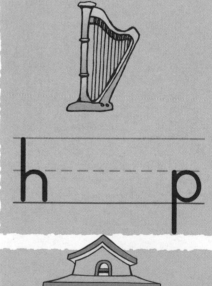

h___p

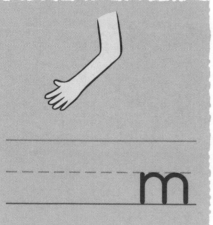

___m

st___

p___ch

r-Controlled Vowels

104

Mix and Match

Name _____

The letters **ur**, **er** and **ir** all have the same sound. Listen for the vowel sound in **surf**, **fern** and **girl**.

s**ur**f    f**er**n   g**ir**l

◆ **Directions:** Draw a line from each word in the circle to the picture it names.

30

herd

turkey

clerk

thirty

purse

bird

105   r-Controlled Vowels

Write ur, er and ir

♦ **Directions:** Find a word from the box to name each picture. Write it on the line below the picture.

church	clerk	dirt	fern
girl	herd	purple	surf	thirty

30

r-Controlled Vowels

Rhyme Time

Name _____

◆ **Directions:** Cut out the words at the bottom of the page. Glue them beside the words they rhyme with.

 barn

 corn

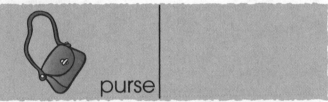 purse

 skirt

 bird

 girl

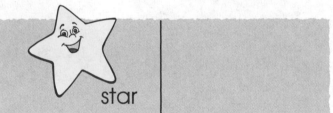 star

 cork

curl   nurse   car   yarn

horn   herd   shirt   fork

r-Controlled Vowels

Vowel Pairs ai and ay

You know that the letters **a_e** usually stand for the long **a** sound. The vowel pairs **ai** and **ay** can stand for the long **a** sound, too. Listen for the long **a** sound in **train** and **hay**.

♦ **Directions:** Say the name of each picture below. Look at the vowel pair that stands for the long **a** sound. Under each picture, write the words from the box that have the same long **a** vowel pair.

cage	chain	gate	gray
mail	pay	snail	skate
play	snake	stay	tail

cake   train   hay

Vowel Pairs

Vowel Pairs oa and ow

Name

You know that the letters **o_e** and **oe** usually stand for the long **o** sound. The vowel pairs **oa** and **ow** can stand for the long **o** sound, too. Listen for the long **o** sound in **road** and **snow**.

♦ **Directions:** Find and circle eight long **o** words. The words may go **across** or **down**. Beside each picture, write the words that use the same long **o** vowel pair.

Z	L	I	A	C	R
B	O	C	R	O	W
S	W	R	J	A	G
O	G	O	A	L	R
A	L	A	G	X	O
P	Y	K	N	O	W

road

snow

Vowel Pair ui

_____
Name

You know that the letters **u_e** and **ue** usually stand for the long **u** sound. The vowel pair **ui** can stand for the long **u** sound, too. Listen for the long **u** sound in **cruise**.

cr**ui**se

♦ **Directions:** Circle the name of the picture.
Then, write the name on the line.

mall
male
mule

_____
- - - - - - - - - - -
_____

sun
Sue
say

_____
- - - - - - - - - - -
_____

fruit
flat
frame

_____
- - - - - - - - - - -
_____

sun
sit
suit

_____
- - - - - - - - - - -
_____

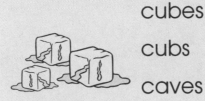

cubes
cubs
caves

_____
- - - - - - - - - - -
_____

Jake
juice
just

_____
- - - - - - - - - - -
_____

fly
flute
fleece

_____
- - - - - - - - - - -
_____

globe
gull
glue

_____
- - - - - - - - - - -
_____

blue
black
ball

_____
- - - - - - - - - - -
_____

Vowel Pairs

Vowel Pair ie

Name

You know that the letters **i_e** usually stand for the long **i** sound. The vowel pair **ie** can stand for the long **i** sound, too. Listen for the long **i** sound in **butterflies**.

butterfli**e**s

♦ **Directions:** Write **i_e** or **ie** to complete each word. Draw a picture for one **i_e** word and one **ie** word.

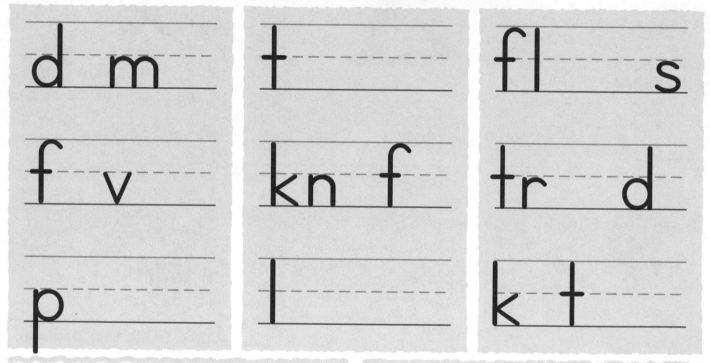

d ___ m	t ___	fl ___ s
f ___ v	kn ___ f	tr ___ d
p ___	l ___	k ___ t

i_e picture

ie picture

Missing Vowel Pairs

♦ **Directions:** Fill in the circle beside the missing vowel pair in each word.

t___	tr___	sn___
○ ie	○ ow	○ ow
○ ay	○ ui	○ ie
○ oa	○ ay	○ ay

ch___n	gr___	r___d
○ ie	○ oa	○ oa
○ ui	○ ay	○ ay
○ ai	○ ie	○ ui

b___	fl___s	s___t
○ ai	○ ai	○ ui
○ ow	○ oa	○ ay
○ ui	○ ie	○ ie

Vowel Pair Review

Missing Vowel Pairs

Name

♦ **Directions:** Fill in the circle beside the missing vowel pair in each word.

h___	tr___n	s___p
○ ui	○ oa	○ oa
○ ow	○ ai	○ ai
○ ay	○ ie	○ ui

j___ce	p___	cr___
○ ai	○ ui	○ ui
○ ui	○ oa	○ ay
○ ie	○ ie	○ ow

g___t	fr___t	sn___l
○ ai	○ ai	○ ow
○ oa	○ ow	○ ai
○ ui	○ ui	○ ie

Vowel Pair ea

Some pairs of vowels can stand for more than one sound. The vowel pair **ea** has the sound of long **e** in **team** and short **e** in **head**.

team  head

♦ **Directions:** Say the name of each picture. Listen for the sound that **ea** stands for. Circle **Long e** or **Short e**. Then, color the pictures whose names have the short **e** sound.

Long e	Short e

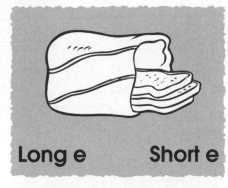

Long e	Short e

Long e	Short e

Long e	Short e

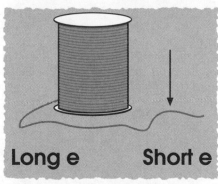

Long e	Short e

Long e	Short e

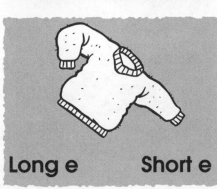

Long e	Short e

Long e	Short e

Long e	Short e

Vowel Pairs

Vowel Pair oo

Listen for the difference between the sound of the vowel pair **oo** in **moon** and its sound in **book**.

moon   book

◆ **Directions:** Say the name of the picture. Circle the picture of the moon or the book to show the sound of vowel pair **oo**.

Make Compound Words

Some short words can be put together to make one new word. The new word is called a **compound word**.

cow + hand = cowhand

♦ **Directions:** Look at each pair of pictures and words below. Join the two words to make a compound word. Write it on the line.

rain + coat = _____

door + bell = _____

dog + house = _____

pan + cake = _____

horse + shoe = _____

Compound Words

Compound Word Riddles

♦ **Directions:** Underline the two words in each sentence that can make a compound word. Write the compound word on the line to complete the sentence.

A kind of bird that is black is a

_____

_____ .

A horse that can race is a

_____

_____ .

A cloth that covers a table is a

_____

_____ .

A room with a bed is a

_____

_____ .

A book with a story is a

_____

_____ .

A bowl that holds fish is a

_____

_____ .

Compound Words   118   © 2001 McGraw Hill Education. All Rights Reserved.

Build Words With Syllables

Name

Syllables are word parts. Each syllable has one vowel sound. Some words have only one syllable. Some words have more than one syllable.

One syllable: kite

Two syllables: wagon

♦ **Directions:** Cut out the syllables at the bottom of the page. Put them together to make eight two-syllable words. Look up the words in a dictionary to check their spellings. Then, write the words you made.

My 2-Syllable Word Record

_____

_____

_____

_____

_____

_____

_____

_____

| pen | der | ket | ro | cil | ster | win | tu |
| dow | bot | bas | kin | lip | spi | mon | nap |

Two-Syllable Words

Prefix re

A **prefix** is a word part. It is added to the beginning of a base word to change the base word's meaning. The prefix **re** means "again."

Example:

Refill means "to fill again."

♦ **Directions:** Look at the pictures. Read the base words. Add the prefix **re** to the base word to show that the action is being done again. Write your new word on the line.

read _____

write _____

paint _____

use _____

build _____

pay _____

Prefixes

Prefixes un and dis

The prefixes **un** and **dis** mean "not" or "the opposite of."

Unlocked means "not locked."

Dismount is the "opposite of mount."

♦ **Directions:** Look at the pictures. Circle the word that tells about the picture. Then, write the word on the line.

tied

untied

_____

like

dislike

_____

happy

unhappy

_____

obey

disobey

_____

safe

unsafe

_____

honest

dishonest

_____

Prefixes

122

Suffixes ful, less, ness, ly

A **suffix** is a word part that is added at the end of a base word to change the base word's meaning. Look at the suffixes below.

The suffix **ful** means "full of." **Cheerful** means "full of cheer."

The suffix **less** means "without." **Cloudless** means "without clouds."

The suffix **ness** means "a state of being." **Darkness** means "being dark."

The suffix **ly** means "in this way." **Slowly** means "in a slow way."

♦ **Directions:** Add the suffixes to the base words to make new words.

care + ful = _____

pain + less = _____

brave + ly = _____

sad + ly = _____

sick + ness = _____

Suffixes

Suffixes and Meanings

Remember: The suffix **ful** means "full of."

The suffix **less** means "without."

The suffix **ness** means "a state of being."

The suffix **ly** means "in this way."

The sun shines **brightly**.

♦ **Directions:** Write the word that matches the meaning.

without pain	in a neat way

full of grace	the state of being sick

in a quick way	without fear

the state of being soft	in a glad way

124

Suffixes er and est

Suffixes **er** and **est** can be used to compare. Use **er** when you compare two things. Use **est** when you compare more than two things.

Example: The puppy is small**er** than its mom.
This puppy is the small**est** puppy in the litter.

♦ **Directions:** Add the suffixes to the base words to make words that compare.

Base Word	+ er	+ est
1. loud	louder	loudest
2. old		
3. neat		
4. fast		
5. kind		
6. tall		

Compare With er and est

Name _____

♦ **Directions:** Use **er** and **est** to compare things in three pictures.

fast _____ _____

loud _____ _____

tall _____ _____

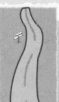

long _____ _____

Suffixes 126 © 2001 McGraw Hill Education. All Rights Reserved.

PHENOMENAL
PHONICS
Award

Awarded to

_____
Name

on _____
Date

**for great
phonics work**

in the
Complete Book of Reading
Grades 1 and 2

Use the Clues

Context clues can help you figure out words you don't know. Read the words around the new word. Think of a word that makes sense.

Kate swam in a _____?_____.

Did Kate swim in a cake or a lake? The word **swim** is a context clue.

♦ **Directions:** Kate wrote this letter from camp. Read the letter. Use context clues to write the missing words from the word box. What clues did you use?

lake	six
pancakes	forest

Dear Mom and Dad,

_____

I woke up at _____ o'clock and got

_____

dressed. My friends and I ate _____ for

_____

breakfast. We went hiking in the _____.

_____

Then, we went swimming in the _____.
Camp is fun!

Love,
Kate

Clues for Clothes

Name _____

♦ **Directions:** Read the story. Use context clues to figure out the missing words. Write the words from the word box. Then, answer the questions.

| socks | scarf | sweaters | mittens |

Maria bundles up. She sticks her arms through

_____

_____

two _____. She tugs three pairs of

_____   _____

_____   _____

_____ over her feet. She wraps a _____

                                     _____

                                     _____

around her neck. At last, she pulls her_____

onto her hands. Maria goes outside to play. Nobody is warmer

than Maria.

1. What clue words helped you figure out sweaters?

_____

_____

2. What clue words helped you figure out mittens?

_____

_____

Context Clues

Context Clues in Action

♦ **Directions:** Read the story. Use context clues to figure out the meanings of the words in dark print. Draw a line from the word to its meaning.

Jack has a plan. He wants to take his parents out to lunch to show that he **appreciates** all the nice things they do for him. His sister Jessica will go, too, so she won't feel left out. Jack is **thrifty**. He saves the **allowance** he earns for doing **chores** around the house. So far, Jack has saved ten dollars. He needs only five dollars more. He is excited about paying the check himself. He will feel like an **adult**.

appreciates	jobs
allowance	grown-up
chores	is grateful for
thrifty	money earned for work
adult	careful about spending money

Amazing Antonyms

Name

Antonyms are words that have opposite meanings. **Old** and **new** are antonyms. **Laugh** and **cry** are antonyms, too.

◆ **Directions:** Below each word, write its antonym. Use words from the word box.

down
go
left
sad
dry

stop

_____

- - - - - - - -

_____

happy

_____

- - - - - - - -

_____

right

_____

- - - - - - - -

_____

up

_____

- - - - - - - -

_____

wet

_____

- - - - - - - -

_____

Antonyms

Scale the Synonym Slope

Name

Synonyms are words that have almost the same meaning. **Tired** and **sleepy** are synonyms. **Talk** and **speak** are synonyms.

♦ **Directions:** Read the word. Find its synonym on the hill. Write the synonym on the line.

1. glad _____

2. little _____

3. begin _____

4. above _____

5. damp _____

6. large _____

wet

big

happy

over

small

start

Synonym Match

Name _____

♦ **Directions:** Look at the pictures. Read the words in the box. Write two synonyms you could use to tell about each picture.

rocks   start   road   begin   street   stones   sad   unhappy

Antonym or Synonym?

Name

♦ **Directions:** Use yellow to color the spaces that have word pairs that are antonyms. Use blue to color the spaces that have word pairs that are synonyms.

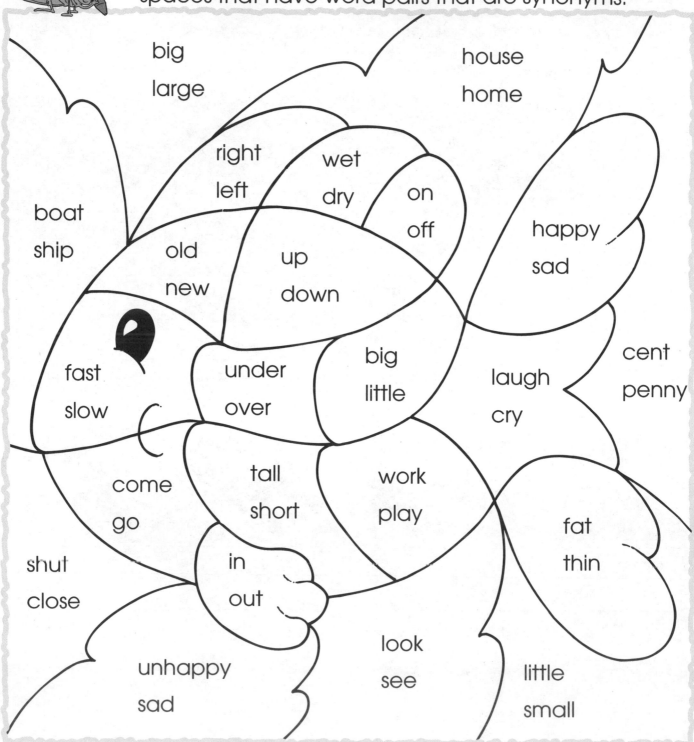

big
large

house
home

right
left

wet
dry

on
off

boat
ship

old
new

up
down

happy
sad

fast
slow

under
over

big
little

laugh
cry

cent
penny

come
go

tall
short

work
play

fat
thin

shut
close

in
out

unhappy
sad

look
see

little
small

Homophone Fun

Homophones are words that sound the same but have different spellings and meanings. **Too** and **two** are homophones. So are **road** and **rode**.

◆ **Directions:** Use yellow to color the balloons that have homophones.

Find the Right Homophone

♦ **Directions:** Read the sentences. Write the correct homophone on the line.

to   two

Jim _____ the cookies.

ate
eight

Sally has _____ pencils.

to
two

The _____ is bumpy.

rode
road

_____ can ride a bike.

Eye
I

Can you _____ the picture?

see
sea

Tom _____ up the balloon.

blew
blue

Homophones   138

Color Code Classifying

♦ **Directions:** Underline **number words** in **red**.
Underline **name words** in **blue**.
Underline **color words** in **green**.
Underline **animal words** in **yellow**.

pig	Kim	dog	blue
red	green	ten	five
Jack	two	cow	Lee

♦ **Directions:** Write each word on the correct line.

Name Words

_____ _____ _____

_____ _____ _____

_____ _____ _____

Number Words

_____ _____ _____

_____ _____ _____

_____ _____ _____

Animal Words

_____ _____ _____

_____ _____ _____

_____ _____ _____

Color Words

_____ _____ _____

_____ _____ _____

_____ _____ _____

Classifying

Menu Mix-Up

♦ **Directions:** Circle **names of vegetables** in **green**.
Circle **names of drinks** in **red**.
Circle **names of desserts** in **pink**.

water

corn
_____
peas

pie

cookie

carrot
_____
cake

juice

milk

menu
drinks
dessert

♦ **Directions:** Write each food word on the correct line.

Drinks	Vegetables	Desserts

Sort It Out

Name _____

◆ **Directions:** Color the pictures. Cut and glue each picture in the correct room.

Bedroom

Bathroom

Kitchen

Classifying

Word Sort

♦ **Directions:** Circle words that name **colors** in **red**.
Circle words that name **shapes** in **yellow**.
Circle words that name **numbers** in **green**.

five   blue

            ten

square   circle

      nine

            purple

      triangle

            brown

♦ **Directions:** Write each word on the correct line.

Colors	Shapes	Numbers

Classifying

Where Does It Belong?

Name

♦ **Directions:** Read the words.
Draw a **circle** around the **sky words**.
Draw a **line** under the **land words**.
Draw a **box** around the **sea words**.

city	rabbit	planet
cloud	forest	whale
shark	moon	shell

♦ **Directions:** Write each word on the correct line.

Sky Words

_____ _____ _____

_____ _____ _____

_____ _____ _____

Land Words

_____ _____ _____

_____ _____ _____

_____ _____ _____

Sea Words

_____ _____ _____

_____ _____ _____

_____ _____ _____

Classifying

144

What's the Big Idea?

Name _____

The **main idea** is the most important idea in a story. The main idea tells what happens.

♦ **Directions:** Look at the pictures. Read the sentences. Circle **yes** if the sentence tells the main idea of the picture. Circle **no** if it does not.

yes   (no)

The hat is too small.

yes   no

The bear is afraid of the mouse.

yes   no

The bear washed three shirts.

yes   no

The circus is fun.

yes   no

The bear has two mittens.

yes   no

The bear walks to school.

Main Idea

Find the Main Idea

Name

♦ **Directions:** Look at the pictures. Read the sentences. In the circle, write the letter of the sentence that tells the main idea.

A. The eggs are ready to hatch.

B. It is a very windy day.

C. The old house looks scary.

D. The popcorn popper is too full.

E. The girl thinks the music is too loud.

F. It is too warm for a snowman.

What's the Idea?

♦ **Directions:** Look at the pictures. Read the sentences in the speech balloons. Fill in the circle beside the sentence that tells the main idea.

My tummy hurts.

○ The mouse wants more to eat.

○ The mouse ate too much cheese.

My hat is blowing away.

○ It is a very windy day.

○ He doesn't want a hat.

I am seven years old today.

○ The cake is very big.

○ Today is her birthday.

I can't find my home.

○ The cat is lost.

○ The cat has a new home.

Main Idea

Read All About It

♦ **Directions:** Read each part of the paper. Fill in the circle beside the sentence that tells the main idea.

Hundreds Enjoy Town Carnival

- ○ Many people had fun at the carnival.
- ○ The carnival was not a success.

- ○ Someone wants to buy kittens and puppies.
- ○ Someone wants to sell kittens and puppies.

CLASSIFIEDS
For Sale
3 black kittens
2 brown puppies
Call 555-4109

Bank Robbers 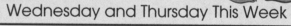 **Caught**

- ○ Five bank robbers got away.
- ○ Two bank robbers were caught.

Garden Club to Meet
Wednesday and Thursday This Week

- ○ The Garden Club will not meet this week.
- ○ The Garden Club will meet two times this week.

Main Idea

148

What Doesn't Belong?

♦ **Directions:** Read the sentences under each title. Cross out the sentence that does not tell about the main idea.

Fun at the Playground

He runs to the slide.

She plays on the swings.

I clean my room.

They climb the monkey bars.

We sit on the seesaw.

Doing My Homework

I open my book.

I take a bath.

I read the book.

I write the words.

I add the numbers.

Going to the Zoo

The monkeys climb the trees.

The seals eat fish.

The snakes move slowly.

The kitten plays with yarn.

The zebra runs fast.

Eating Dinner

Mother cuts the meat.

Father chews the corn.

Sister drinks the milk.

Brother eats his peas.

Grandmother has a big house.

Main Idea

Main Ideas About Meals

Name

♦ **Directions:** Read each story to find the main idea. Fill in the circle beside the phrase that tells the main idea.

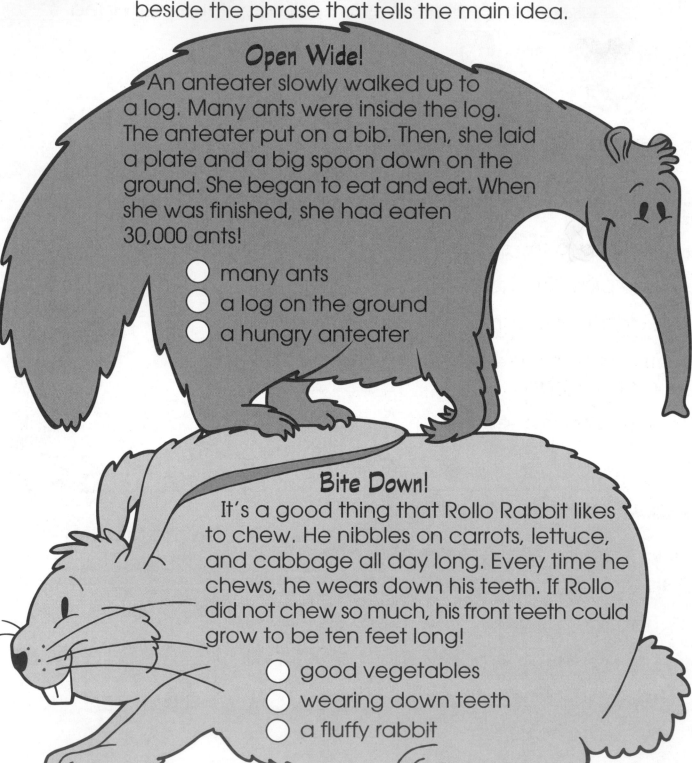

Open Wide!

An anteater slowly walked up to a log. Many ants were inside the log. The anteater put on a bib. Then, she laid a plate and a big spoon down on the ground. She began to eat and eat. When she was finished, she had eaten 30,000 ants!

○ many ants
○ a log on the ground
○ a hungry anteater

Bite Down!

It's a good thing that Rollo Rabbit likes to chew. He nibbles on carrots, lettuce, and cabbage all day long. Every time he chews, he wears down his teeth. If Rollo did not chew so much, his front teeth could grow to be ten feet long!

○ good vegetables
○ wearing down teeth
○ a fluffy rabbit

Main Idea

Storyboard Sequence

Name

Sequence is the order in which story events happen. What happened first? What happened next? What happened last?

♦ **Directions:** Write the numbers 1, 2 and 3 in the boxes to show the order in which the story events in each row happened.

Sequence

Words in Order

♦ **Directions:** Look at each picture. Write 1, 2 and 3 to make the words tell a story in order.

☐ mix

☐ eat

☐ bake

☐ give

☐ open

☐ buy

☐ fly

☐ land

☐ take off

☐ read

☐ open

☐ close

☐ listen

☐ turn off

☐ turn on

☐ hurt

☐ fall

☐ bandage

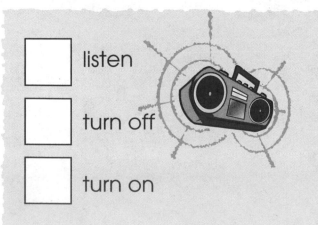

Sequence

152

Story Sequence

♦ **Directions:** Read the story.

Over a hundred years ago, two men built a town. They couldn't decide what to name it. One man wanted to name it Boston. The other wanted to name it Portland. They tossed a coin and one yelled, "Heads for Boston!" The other yelled, "Tails for Portland!" Tails must have won because that town is now called Portland, Oregon.

♦ **Directions:** Read the sentences. Write 1, 2, 3 and 4 to number the events in the order they happened in the story.

built a town.

STABLE	HOTEL	GENERAL STORE	JAIL
The town is now called Portland.	They could not decide what to name the town.	Two men	They tossed a coin.

153

Sequence

Otter Order

Name

♦ **Directions:** Read the story.

A sea otter eats clams, barnacles, worms, sea urchins and abalone. First, it must dive underwater to find its food. After bringing the food to the surface, the sea otter rolls onto its back and puts the food on its belly. It keeps its "picnic table" clean by rolling in the water to wash away any messy scraps. Sea otters are very neat eaters!

♦ **Directions:** Write the number 1, 2, 3, 4 or 5 in each box to tell the order in which the sea otter eats a meal.

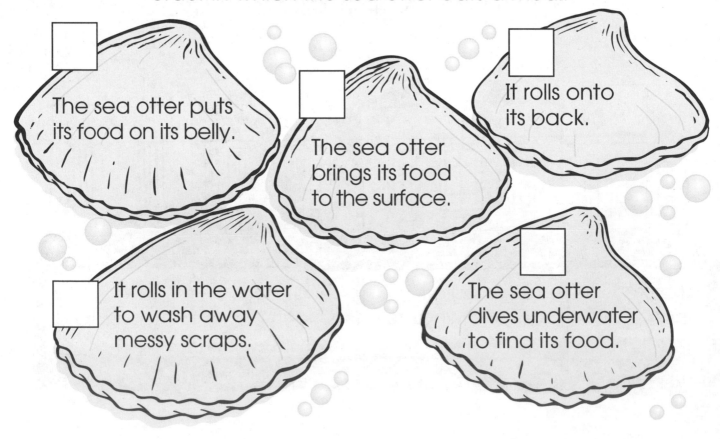

The sea otter puts its food on its belly.

The sea otter brings its food to the surface.

It rolls onto its back.

It rolls in the water to wash away messy scraps.

The sea otter dives underwater to find its food.

Lemonade for Sale

Name

♦ **Directions:** Read the story.

Ken and Pat start a business selling lemonade. First, they make a stand from Pat's picnic table. Second, they go to the store to buy a box of lemons and a sack of sugar. Third, they squeeze the lemons and pick out the seeds. Fourth, they mix the lemon juice with sugar and cold water. Would you like to buy a cold glass of lemonade from them? It's only fifteen cents.

♦ **Directions:** Read the phrases. Write 1, 2, 3 and 4 to number the phrases in the order they happened in the story. Clue words like **first** will help you.

☐ buy lemons and sugar

☐ make a stand

☐ mix lemon juice, sugar and water

☐ squeeze lemons and pick out seeds

♦ **Directions:** On another sheet of paper, write what you think Ken and Pat will do next.

 155

Sequence

A Hare-Raising Experience

♦ **Directions:** Read the story.

Jack Rabbit loved to grow carrots. First, he found a diamond-shaped field. Next, he carefully planted and watered the seeds. Then he watched as the little green tops of carrots began pushing through the dirt. Finally, 83 carrots were ready to be pulled from the earth. Jack indeed had the only 83-"carrot" diamond in town, and he proudly gave it to his friend Jill.

♦ **Directions:** Read the sentences. Write 1, 2, 3, 4 or 5 to number the sentences in the order they happened in the story.

☐ The carrots were ready to be pulled.

☐ Carrot tops started popping up.

☐ Jack found a field.

☐ Jack watered the seeds.

☐ Jack planted carrot seeds.

♦ **Directions:** On another sheet of paper, write what you think will happen next.

Sequence

 156

Fun With Directions

◆ **Directions:** Follow the number code to color the balloons.
Color the clown, too.

1 — blue	2 — orange	3 — yellow	4 — green	5 — purple
6 — brown	7 — red	8 — black	9 — blue	10 — purple

Following Directions

Draw With Directions

♦ **Directions:** Follow the directions to complete the picture.

1. Draw a smiling yellow face on the sun.

2. Color the fish blue. Draw 2 more blue fish in the water.

3. Draw a brown bird under the cloud. Draw blue raindrops under the cloud.

4. Color the boat purple. Color one sail orange. Color the other sail green.

5. Color the starfish yellow. Draw 2 more yellow starfish.

Directions for Decorating

♦ **Directions:** Follow the directions to decorate the bedroom.

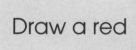 Draw a red 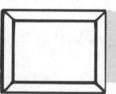 between the two .

 Draw a chair under the window. Color it green.

 Draw three big flowers on the wall. Color them orange.

Draw a picture of something you would like to have in your bedroom.

 Following Directions

Follow the Course

Name _____

♦ **Directions:** Tear out page 161. Place a penny in the top left corner. Then, follow the directions below to win the trophy. Check off the directions as you follow them.

1. ☐ Go right 7 spaces.
   ☐ Go down 5 spaces.
   ☐ Go left 6 spaces.
   ☐ Go down 4 spaces.
   ☐ Leap through the hoop.

2. ☐ Go right 3 spaces.
   ☐ Go up 5 spaces.
   ☐ Go left 4 spaces.
   ☐ Go up 1 space.
   ☐ Do a handstand on your skateboard.

3. ☐ Go right 2 spaces.
   ☐ Go up 2 spaces.
   ☐ Go right 3 spaces.
   ☐ Go down 3 spaces.
   ☐ Glide down the ramp.

4. ☐ Go right 1 space.
   ☐ Go down 3 spaces.
   ☐ Go left 3 spaces.
   ☐ Go down 2 spaces.
   ☐ Turn the corner.

5. ☐ Go right 4 spaces.
   ☐ Go up 8 spaces.
   ☐ Go left 4 spaces.
   ☐ Go down 1 space.
   ☐ Duck! Here's a tunnel.

6. ☐ Go left 2 spaces.
   ☐ Go down 6 spaces.
   ☐ Go left 1 space.
   ☐ Go up 2 spaces.
   ☐ You made it! Collect your trophy.

Skateboard Course

Name _____

What Is It?

When you don't get the whole picture, you may need to **draw conclusions** for yourself. To draw a conclusion, think about what you see or read. Think about what you already know. Then, make a good guess.

♦ **Directions:** Look at each picture. Use what you know and what you see to draw a conclusion. Draw a line to the sentence that tells about each picture.

It must be a clown.

It must be a cowhand.

It must be a baby.

It must be a ballet dancer.

It must be a football player.

163

Drawing Conclusions

Who Said It?

Name

♦ **Directions:** Use what you see, what you read and what you know to draw conclusions. Draw a line from the animal to what it might say.

"I save lots of bones and bury them in the yard."

"I live in the ocean and have sharp teeth."

"I love to walk in the snow and slide on the ice."

"I hop on lily pads in a pond with my webbed feet."

"I slither on the ground because I have no arms or legs."

Drawing Conclusions

What Happened?

Name _____

♦ **Directions:** Look at the pictures. Fill in the circle beside the sentence that tells what happened in the missing picture. Draw a picture that shows what happened.

What happened?

○ The boy dropped the string.　　○ The boy took his kite home.

What happened?

○ The angry baby played in its bed.　　○ The hungry baby drank the milk.

Drawing Conclusions

♦ **Directions:** Read the sentences. Look at the pictures. Circle the picture that completes the last sentence.

1. Emily is on a class trip. She sees cows eating grass and horses in the barn. Hens are sitting on their eggs. She must be visiting a . . .

2. Timmy wore his best suit. He sat in a tall chair. He combed his hair. A man said, "Say cheese!" The man is a . . .

3. Mark spilled milk on the floor. He had to clean up the mess. He went to the closet and got a . . .

I Conclude!

♦ **Directions:** Read each story. Fill in the circle beside the answer that completes the last sentence.

The little house is in the backyard. Inside is a bowl of water. Next to the bowl is a big bone. This house belongs to . . .

○ some birds.   ○ a family of elves.   ○ a puppy.

The yellow cat is fluffy. The black cat is thin. The tan and white cat acts friendly. The little gray cat is shy. Cats are all . . .

○ different.   ○ angry.   ○ silly.

Lois keeps her pet in an aquarium. Her pet can hop. It eats flies and is green. Her pet is . . .

○ a bunny.   ○ a frog.   ○ very tall.

We played a game. We ran away from Sofia. When she tapped Raymond, he was It. We were playing . . .

○ soccer.   ○ basketball.   ○ tag.

Drawing Conclusions

Clues to Conclusions

♦ **Directions:** Read each story. Fill in the circle beside the correct conclusion.

Joe tried to read the book. He pulled it closer to his face and squinted. What is wrong?

- ○ The book isn't very interesting.
- ○ Joe needs glasses.
- ○ The book is closed.

"My shoes are too tight," said Eddie, "and my pants are too short!" What has happened?

- ○ Eddie has put on his older brother's clothes.
- ○ Eddie has become shorter.
- ○ Eddie has grown.

Patsy went to the beach. She stayed outside for hours. When she came home, she looked in the mirror. Her face was very red. Why did she look different?

- ○ Patsy had gotten a bad sunburn.
- ○ Patsy got red paint all over herself.
- ○ Patsy was very cold.

Drawing Conclusions

Find the Facts

Facts and details tell more about the main idea. Facts and details give more information.

Small, brown, long-haired dog
Wearing blue collar with tag
Last seen on May 12

If you find Rowdy, please call 555-6702 or bring him to 436 West London Street. Ask for Donna.

♦ **Directions:** Read the poster. Answer the questions.

1. What color is the pet? _____

2. What is the owner's name? _____

3. What is the pet's name? _____

4. Where does the pet live? _____

_____

169

Facts and Details

Facts About Fingerprints

♦ **Directions:** Read the story.

   The lines and swirls on your fingertips make fingerprints. There are three fingerprint patterns. The first is called the loop. The second is the arch. The third is the whorl. Your fingerprints stay the same all your life. Each person's fingerprints are different.

loop

arch   whorl

♦ **Directions:** Read each sentence. Color the **True** ink pad if the sentence is true. Color the **False** ink pad if the sentence is false.

1. There are four fingerprint patterns.

   True   False

2. Your fingerprints change as you grow.

   True   False

3. Fingerprints are made from the lines and swirls on your fingertips.

   True   False

4. No one else has fingerprints exactly like yours.

   True   False

Facts and Details

Pictures in Detail

◆ **Directions:** Read the story.

The Aztecs in Mexico used straw to make pictures. First, they colored the straw using dyes made from plants. Next, they drew a design. Then, they cut the straw into small pieces. Finally, they glued each piece of straw to the design to form the picture.

◆ **Directions:** Complete the sentences with words from the story.

1. Aztecs in _____ used straw to make

_____

_____ .

2. Dyes were made from _____ .

3. The _____ was cut into small pieces.

4. Each piece was _____ to the _____ .

Facts and Details

Details Wanted!

Here is a wanted poster about One-Eyed Harry who robbed a bank last night. Harry has a mean and beady eye. He wears a patch over his other eye just to scare people. He's about five feet tall and wears a polka-dot bandanna. He has a dirty beard and a long pointed nose with a wart on the tip. He wears an earring in one ear, and he has one gold front tooth.

Wanted

One-Eyed Harry

♦ **Directions:** Circle **Yes** or **No** to tell about the details.

Harry wears a polka-dot bandanna.	Yes	No
Harry has two kind eyes.	Yes	No
Harry has a long pointed nose.	Yes	No
Harry wears an earring in his nose.	Yes	No
Harry has a gold front tooth.	Yes	No

Facts and Details

Same and Different

Name

Reading to find out how things are **alike** or **different** can help you picture and remember what you read. Things that are alike are called **similarities**. Things that are not alike are called **differences**.

Similarity: Beth and Michelle are both girls.
Difference: Beth has short hair, but Michelle has long hair.

◆ **Directions:** Read the story.

Michelle and Beth are wearing new dresses. Both dresses are striped and have four shiny buttons. Each dress has a belt and a pocket. Beth's dress is blue and white, while Michelle's is yellow and white. The stripes on Beth's dress go up and down. Stripes on Michelle's dress go from side to side. Beth's pocket is bigger with room for a kitten.

◆ **Directions:** Add the details. Color the dresses. Show how the dresses are alike and how they are different.

Beth's Dress	Michelle's Dress
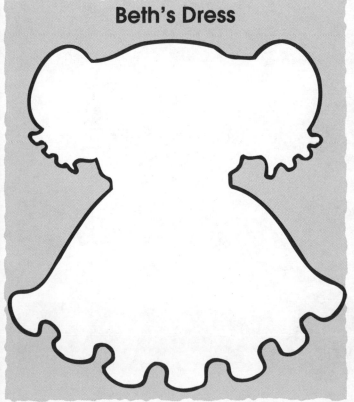	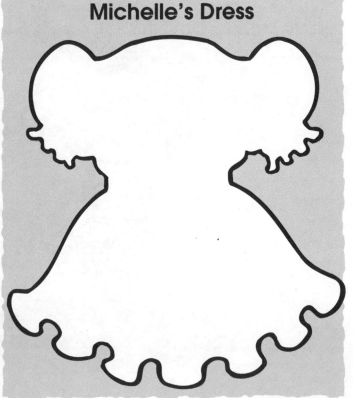

Similarities and Differences

Comparing Cars

♦ **Directions:** Read the story.

Sarah built a car for a race. Sarah's car has wheels, a steering wheel and a place to sit just like the family car. It doesn't have a motor, a key or a gas pedal. Sarah came in second in last year's race. This year, she hopes to win the race.

♦ **Directions:** Write **S** beside the things Sarah's car has that are like things the family car has. Write **D** beside the things that are different.

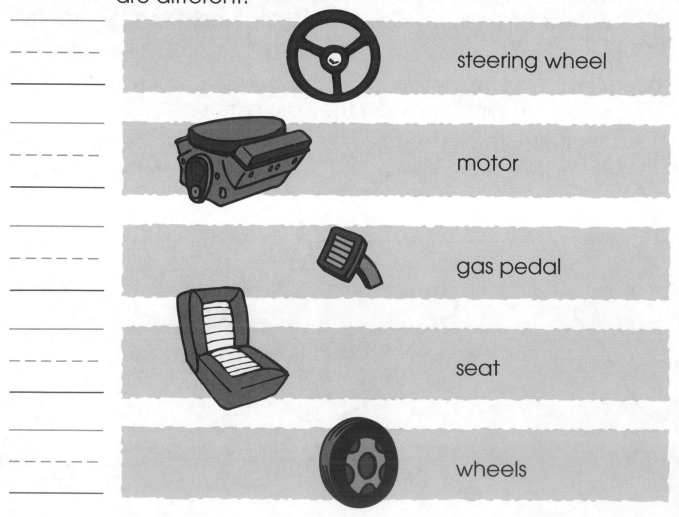

steering wheel

motor

gas pedal

seat

wheels

Similarities and Differences

174

Alike and Different

A Cut and Fold Book

♦ **Directions:** The pages of your Cut and Fold Book are on the back of this sheet. First, follow the directions below to make the book. Then, read your book to a family member or friend. Think of other things that are alike and different.

1. Tear the page out of the book.

2. Fold page along Line A so that the top meets the bottom. Make sure Line A is on the outside of the fold.

LINE A

3. Fold along Line B to make the book.

   Similarities and Differences

He is sad.

He is happy.

Line B

Line A

She is short.

She is tall.

The elephant is big.

The mouse is little.

ALIKE AND DIFFERENT
A CUT AND FOLD BOOK

Making Inferences

Not every story tells you all the facts. Sometimes you need to put together details to understand what is happening in a story. When you put details together, you **make inferences**.

♦ **Directions:** Read each story. Fill in the circle beside the inference you can make from the details you have.

Everyone on the Pine School baseball team wears a blue shirt on Mondays. It is Monday and Brenda is wearing a blue shirt.

- ○ Brenda always wears blue clothes.
- ○ Brenda cannot find her red shirt.
- ○ Brenda is on the baseball team.

My cat has brown and white stripes. It meows when it wants to be fed. My cat is meowing now.

- ○ The cat wants to go outside.
- ○ The cat is hungry.
- ○ The cat doesn't like brown and white stripes.

Every afternoon the children run outside when they hear a bell ring. At 2:00, Mr. Chocovan drives by in his ice-cream truck. The children hear a bell ringing. They run outside.

- ○ It is time for ice cream.
- ○ It is time for the children to go home.
- ○ It is time for a fire drill.

Making Inferences

Figure It Out

♦ **Directions:** Read the story.

It is a rainy day. Mom tells Tosh to stay inside until the weather clears up. Tosh lies on his bed and pouts. He sings one song over and over. Now and then, he checks to see if the rain has stopped.

♦ **Directions:** Use details in the story to make inferences. Fill in the circle beside the phrase that completes each sentence.

Tosh probably wants to   ○ go outside and play.

○ lie in bed all day.

Tosh probably feels   ○ happy.

○ bored and grumpy.

The song Tosh probably sings is   ○ "Rain, Rain, Go Away."

○ "Jingle Bells."

Making Inferences

Inferences About Characters

Name

♦ **Directions:** Read this story. Look for clues about Tom. Then, follow the directions below the story.

"You can't get me!" Goldie teased Tom when she saw him looking at her.

"I never said that I wanted to get you, anyway," answered Tom, knowing that Goldie was right. He walked away, waving his fluffy tail proudly.

Although Goldie had once been afraid of Tom, she now liked to tease him.

"It's fun to tease Tom. When he is upset, all his fur stands straight up," she thought.

Soon Goldie heard noises. Someone else was home. "It is almost time for dinner," thought Goldie. "I'm really glad to be a goldfish. I'm safe and sound and very well fed."

What does Tom look like? Draw a picture of Tom.

Circle the picture that tells how Goldie feels.

Making Inferences

Mind-Reading Tricks

Samantha thought of a good joke. She bragged that she could read Maria's mind. She put her hand on Maria's head, closed her eyes, and said, "You had red punch with your lunch!"

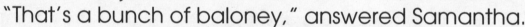

"Wow! You're right!" replied Maria, not realizing that she had a little red ring around her lips.

"That was easy. But I bet you can't tell me what I just ate," said Thomas.

"That's a bunch of baloney," answered Samantha.

"How did you know?" gasped Thomas.

"It's my little secret," said Samantha, with a sigh of relief.

"Here comes your mom," said Maria. "Can you read her mind, too?"

Samantha looked down at her watch. She should have been home half an hour ago. As she ran to meet her mother, she yelled back, "Yes, I know exactly what she's thinking!"

◆ **Directions:** Make inferences about Samantha's mind-reading tricks. Fill in the circle beside the correct inference.

1. Was Samantha sure that Thomas had eaten bologna for lunch?

   ◯ No, she was just lucky.

   ◯ Yes, she saw him eat his bologna sandwich.

2. What was Samantha's mother probably thinking?

   ◯ Samantha was a great mind reader.

   ◯ Samantha was late.

Making Inferences

 180

Tricky Cause and Effect

Name

Things that happen can make other things happen. The event that happens is the **effect**. Why the event happens is the **cause**.

Example: Marcie tripped on the step and fell down.
Cause: Marcie tripped on the step.
Effect: Marcie fell down.

♦ **Directions:** Read the story.

Marcie knows a magic trick. She can make a ring seem to go up and down by itself on a pencil. Marcie has to get ready ahead of time. She ties a piece of skinny thread under the pencil's eraser. Then, she ties the thread to a button on her blouse. In front of her audience, Marcie puts a ring on the pencil. When Marcie leans forward, the thread goes loose, so the ring goes down. Then, Marcie leans back. The thread tightens and makes the ring go up the pencil.

♦ **Directions:** Write the cause to complete each sentence.

1. The audience cannot see the thread because

_____

_ _

_____

_____

2. _

_____

makes the ring go down.

Cause and Effect

Why Did It Happen?

Directions: Read the effects. Fill in the circle beside the sentence that tells what caused the effect.

The soccer coach is cheering.

○ Her team lost the game.

○ Her team won the game.

Patty found only one cookie in the cookie jar.

○ Someone ate all the other cookies.

○ It was a brand new cookie jar.

Fred has a new pair of glasses.

○ Fred was having trouble seeing the chalkboard.

○ There was a sale on glasses.

Lynn turned the fan to high.

○ It was a very cold day.

○ It was a very hot day.

Jason took his umbrella to school.

○ The sky was cloudy.

○ The sun was shining.

Cause and Effect

182

Chain of Effects

Name _____

◆ **Directions:** Read the story.

At night, Tran set his alarm clock for seven o'clock. When it rang the next morning, he was so tired he turned the alarm off. Then, he went back to sleep. Tran finally woke up at eight o'clock. Tran had missed the school bus. He had to walk to school. It was a long walk. Tran was very late!

◆ **Directions:** Draw a line to match a cause to an effect.

Because he was tired,

Because Tran turned off the alarm,

Because he woke up at eight o'clock,

Because Tran missed the bus,

Because he had a long walk,

Tran missed the school bus.

he had to walk to school.

Tran turned off the alarm.

Tran was late for school.

he overslept.

Cause and Effect

A Cause and Effect Fable

Name

♦ **Directions:** Read the story.

Four animals caught a talking fish.
"If you let me go, I will grant each
of you one wish," announced the fish.
"Make my trunk smaller!"
demanded the vain elephant. "I wish
to be the most beautiful elephant
that ever lived."
"Make my legs longer!"
commanded the alligator. "I want to
be taller than all my alligator friends."
"Make my neck shorter!" ordered the giraffe. "I am tired of always
staring at the tops of trees."
"Dear Fish, please make me be satisfied with who-o-o-o-o I am,"
whispered the wise old owl.
Poof! Kazaam! Their wishes were granted. However, soon after,
only one of these animals was happy. Can you guess who-o-o-o-o?

♦ **Directions:** Draw a line to match a cause to an effect.

Because of its short trunk,	the giraffe could no longer eat leaves from treetops.
Because of its long legs,	the elephant could no longer spray water on its back.
Because of its short neck,	the owl was happy about his wish.
Because he could still do all the things he needed,	the alligator could no longer hide in shallow water.

Cause and Effect

 184

What Comes Next?

It's fun to try to guess what will happen next as you read. Guessing what will happen is called **predicting outcomes**.

What you read: Liz drops the glass vase.

What you can predict: The glass vase will break.

♦ **Directions:** Read the story. Then, follow the directions below.

Every Saturday, Grace cleans her room. One Saturday, Grace forgot to clean it because she was busy playing with her cat, Tiger. Mom looked in and saw that Grace's room was still messy.

1. Complete the sentence to make a prediction.

_____

Now, Grace will probably _____

_____

_____

2. Color the things Grace will probably hang in her closet.

Predicting Outcomes

What Will They Do?

◆ **Directions:** Read each sentence. Fill in the circle beside the best prediction. Then, circle the picture that matches your answer.

The boy is putting on his skates.

○ He will go swimming.

○ He will go skating.

The girl fills her glass with milk.

○ She will drink the milk.

○ She will drink water.

The woman wrote a letter to her friend.

○ She will call her friend on the phone.

○ She will put the letter in the mailbox.

The kids gave Sally a birthday gift.

○ She will open the gift.

○ She will throw the gift away.

Predicting Outcomes

 186

Pup Predictions

Name _____

♦ **Directions:** Read the story.

When Donald tells Dudley to sit, Dudley rolls over. If Donald asks him to come, Dudley runs away. To surprise Dad, Donald tries to teach Dudley to fetch the newspaper. Dudley rips it up! Donald will take Dudley to dog obedience school.

♦ **Directions:** Make predictions. Draw three things Dudley will probably learn in obedience school.

Predicting Outcomes

How Will It End?

♦ **Directions:** Read each story. Fill in the circle beside the sentence that tells what will happen next.

It is a snowy winter night. The lights flicker once, twice, and then they go out. It is cold and dark. Dad finds the flashlight and matches. He brings logs in from outside. What will Dad do?

○ Dad will make a fire.

○ Dad will cook dinner.

○ Dad will clean the fireplace.

Maggie has a garden. She likes fresh, homegrown vegetables. She says they make salads taste better. Maggie is going to make a salad for a picnic. What will Maggie do?

○ Maggie will buy the salad at the store.

○ Maggie will buy the vegetables at the store.

○ Maggie will use vegetables from her garden.

The big white goose wakes up. It stands and stretches its wings. It looks all around. It feels very hungry. What will the goose do?

○ The goose will go swimming.

○ The goose will look for food.

○ The goose will go back to sleep.

188

Five Polliwogs

A Cut and Fold Book

♦ **Directions:** The pages of your Cut and Fold Book are on the back of this sheet. First, follow the directions below to make the book. Next, color the pictures. Then, read the story to a family member or friend. Stop reading after page three. Ask your listener to predict what will happen next. Then, finish reading the story.

1. Tear the page out of the book.

2. Fold page along Line A so that the top meets the bottom. Make sure Line A is on the outside of the fold.

3. Fold along Line B to make the book.

189

Predicting Outcomes

The fourth one said, "My legs are getting strong."

The fifth one said, "It will not be very long."

Line B

Line A

The second one said, "I have a funny tail."

The third one said, "And a tail can help me sail."

Five Polliwogs

Five polliwogs swam near the shore.

The first one said, "I have never been this way before."

1

Five polliwogs deep in the bog.

Each gave a croak and became a frog.

4

You Be the Judge

Story characters often have to make choices. As the reader, you decide whether or not the choices are good ones. This is called **making judgments**.

♦ **Directions:** Read the story.

On his way home from the park, Jason finds a baseball mitt under a bush. Alan tells Jason to keep the mitt because he is the one who found it. Arnold tells him to leave it there. Austin tells Jason to take it to the Lost and Found Department at the park. Jason looks inside the mitt. He can see a name and a telephone number.

Alan   Austin   Jason   Arnold

♦ **Directions:** Answer the questions.

1. Who do you think gave the best advice? _____

_____

_____

2. What do you think Jason should do? _____

_____

_____

_____

_____

Making Judgments

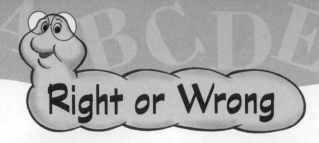

Right or Wrong

♦ **Directions:** Read the story.

Today is Karl's day to have the ball at lunch recess. Danny forgets it is Karl's turn and takes the ball outside. Karl asks Danny for the ball. Danny won't give it to him. Karl grabs the ball from Danny and runs away from him.

♦ **Directions:** Make judgments about what each boy did wrong. Write a new ending for the story. Show how the boys could solve their problem without fighting.

Today is Karl's day to have the ball at lunch recess. Danny forgets it is Karl's turn and takes the ball outside. Karl asks Danny for the ball.

_____

- -

_____

- -

_____

- -

_____

- -

_____

Making Judgments

Judge for Yourself

Name

♦ **Directions:** Read the story.

Arnold the Bully is trying to make friends. He isn't sure what he should do because he has always been a bully. He tries to buy friends by giving away his lunch and his toys. He listens to kids and doesn't boss them around. He takes turns and doesn't call names. He brags about what his dad does at work.

♦ **Directions:** Read each of Arnold's choices. Fill in the circle to show whether you think the choice is good or bad.

1. Arnold tries to buy friends.   ○ Good   ○ Bad

2. Arnold listens to what kids say.   ○ Good   ○ Bad

3. Arnold doesn't boss kids around.   ○ Good   ○ Bad

4. Arnold takes turns.   ○ Good   ○ Bad

5. Arnold doesn't call names.   ○ Good   ○ Bad

6. Arnold brags about his dad.   ○ Good   ○ Bad

               Making Judgments

Which Brand Is the Best?

♦ **Directions:** Read the story.

Randy takes Pixie to the store to buy a big bag of dog food. All the dog food makers say their dog food is the best. The makers of Good Stuff say their food will give dogs longer lives. Best Ever dog food says it gives the extra vitamins dogs need for strong bones and teeth. Bits and Bits says it will give dogs good health and no bad dog breath.

♦ **Directions:** Fill in the circle beside the name of each person who would probably give Randy good advice about choosing a dog food.

○ vet

○ cat lover

○ clerk selling Bits and Bits

○ dog breeder

Making Judgments

Realistic Story or Fantasy?

Many stories are made-up stories. A made-up story about things that could really happen is a **realistic story**. Some made-up stories, such as fairy tales, tell about things that could never really happen. Those stories are **fantasies**.

Realistic Story: A girl hits a home run and wins the game for her team.

Fantasy: A girl hits the ball. It sprouts wings and flies away on an adventure.

◆ **Directions:** Read the book reviews. Fill in the circle to show whether each story is a realistic story or a fantasy.

The Flying Hippo is about a hippo that flies through the sky. He lands at a busy airport and wanders through New York City.

○ Realistic story   ○ Fantasy

A Goose Learns to Fly is about a family who saves an injured baby goose. Later, they teach it to fly on its own.

○ Realistic story   ○ Fantasy

The First Airplane is about the Wright Brothers and the airplane they invented.

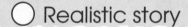

○ Realistic story   ○ Fantasy

The Magic Airplane is about a toy airplane that flies to the planet Mars.

○ Realistic story   ○ Fantasy

Realism or Fantasy?

Fantasy Tales

Name _____

If even one thing in a story could not really happen, the whole story is a fantasy.

♦ **Directions:** Read the stories. Underline the sentence that makes each story a fantasy.

Michelle got a kitten for her birthday. It was soft and cuddly. It liked to chase fuzzy toys. After playing, it napped in Michelle's lap. One day the kitten said to Michelle, "Would you like me to tell you a story?"

The team lined up. The kicker kicked the football. Up, up it soared. It went up so high that it went into orbit around the Earth. The game was over. The Aardvarks had won.

"This is a great car," the salesperson said. "It can go very fast. It can cook your breakfast. It always starts, even on the coldest day. You really should buy this car."

Chris studied about healthy food in school. He learned that milk could make him grow. Chris drank a glass of milk just before he went to bed. When he got up in the morning, he was so tall, his head went right through the ceiling.

Write About Reality

♦ **Directions:** Write a journal entry. Write about a special day. You can make up the story, but make sure everything you write is something that could really happen.

Realism or Fantasy?

Write a Fantasy

♦ **Directions:** Write a new journal entry. Write about the same special day you wrote about on page 197. This time, add details to make your story a fantasy.

_____

_____

_____

_____

_____

_____

_____

_____

_____

_____

_____

_____

_____

_____

_____

_____

_____

_____

Realism or Fantasy?

Know Your Characters

Name _____

Characters are the people or animals in a story. Understanding characters in a story helps you understand what happens. As you read, think about how you would act if you were the character. Think about how you would feel.

◆ **Directions:** Look at the pictures. Write words from the box to name the character's feelings.

glad	unhappy	pleased
sorry	sad	happy

_____

_ _ _ _ _ _ _ _ _ _ _ _ _ _ _ _

_____

_ _ _ _ _ _ _ _ _ _ _ _ _ _ _ _

_____

_ _ _ _ _ _ _ _ _ _ _ _ _ _ _ _

_____

Appreciating Literature

Characters' Feelings

Name _____

◆ **Directions:** Read the first sentence. Use a word from below to complete the second sentence. Draw the correct expression on the character's face.

surprised

sad

angry

Eric's best friend moves to a new town.

_____

- -

He feels _____ .

A big bully pulls Julia's hair.

_____

- -

She feels _____ .

On Saturday, Harry sees a magic show.

_____

- -

He feels _____ .

Appreciating Literature

 200

Emotion Search

◆ **Directions:** Check the happy words. Circle them in the word search. The words go **across** and **down**.

☐ jolly   ☐ sick   ☐ friendly

☐ pleased   ☐ scared   ☐ surprised

☐ lucky   ☐ proud   ☐ sorry

☐ mad   ☐ brave   ☐ excited

```
F  B  J  O  F  U  S  C  A
S  U  R  P  R  I  S  E  D
H  V  L  U  I  R  R  Y  E
N  A  P  L  E  A  S  E  D
G  L  J  K  N  C  P  M  O
Y  P  O  A  D  L  X  A  L
B  R  L  O  L  U  C  K  Y
K  O  L  T  Y  Z  Q  J  O
A  U  Y  U  O  E  T  P  L
K  D  B  R  A  V  E  S  I
E  X  C  I  T  E  D  E  M
```

201

Appreciating Literature

♦ **Directions:** Read the story.

Yesterday, my friend Rex and I visited the museum. We were excited about seeing the new dinosaur display.

"Wow!" I yelled when I looked up at the tyrannosaurus skeleton.

"He's my distant cousin," Rex joked. "In fact, I was named after him!"

"My cousin was really a picky eater," giggled Rex. "He's no skin, just bones!"

That night, I dreamed of that tyrannosaurus. I imagined him sticking his head into my bedroom window. I was too frightened to scream. When he opened his huge mouth, I froze.

"Do you know what happened to me because I wouldn't take a bath?" thundered the dinosaur.

I shook my head.

"I became x-stinked!" he roared.

Now, I think that Rex and his dinosaur "cousin" must really be related. They both tell bad jokes!

♦ **Directions:** Both Rex and his "cousin" like telling jokes. Circle the five words below that best describe the "cousins."

sad	silly	funny
jolly	brave	
comical	pranksters	

Plot and Setting

Stories have a setting and a plot. The **setting** tells where and when the story takes place. The **plot** tells what happened.

♦ **Directions:** Read the story. Then, follow the directions below.

Michael, Sam and Dominic were best friends. They ate lunch together. At recess, they swung on the swings together. On the swings, Michael said, "Come to my house to play after school." Dominic thought Michael was looking at Sam. He waited for Michael to ask him, too, but Michael didn't. All afternoon, Dominic felt sad. When the bell rang, he started to go home. "Where are you going?" Michael called. "I wanted you both to come to my house." With a big smile, Dominic ran to join Michael and Sam.

Fill in the circle beside the words that tell about the story's setting.

- ○ After school at Sam's house
- ○ At school on a school day
- ○ At the park on a Saturday

Number the plot events to show the order in which they happened.

- ☐ Dominic felt sad because he thought he wasn't invited.

- ☐ Dominic and Sam went to Michael's house.

- ☐ Michael invited the boys over.

Appreciating Literature

What's the Story?

Name

♦ **Directions:** Read the story.

Jimmy hid a rubber spider inside Ronald's desk. Ronald yelled when he opened his desk to get a book. Then, Ronald put the rubber spider in the sink. Tammy squealed when she bent down to get a drink. Finally, Tammy put the rubber spider inside Jimmy's tennis shoe. Jimmy screamed loudest of all when he saw it. The other kids giggled.

♦ **Directions:** Use the story map to tell what happened in the story. Draw a picture of the spider in each place it was hidden. Draw the pictures in order.

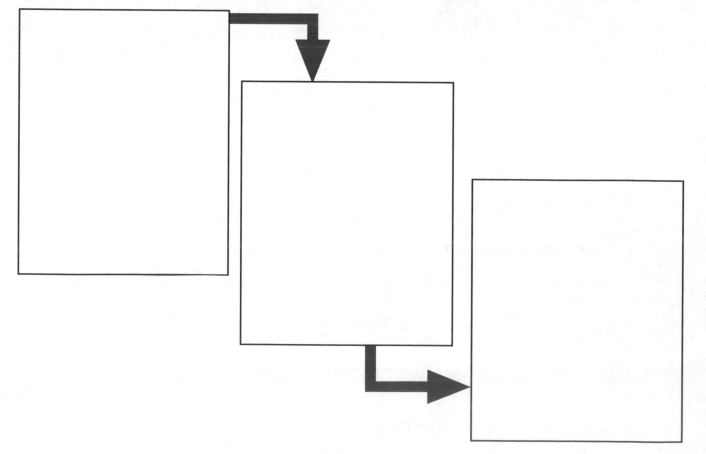

Do It Yourself Setting

When   Where

♦ **Directions:** Cut out each phrase. Sort the phrases into two stacks. Make one stack for phrases that tell when. Make another stack for phrases that tell where. Choose a card from each stack. Write or tell a story that has the setting the cards show.

before dinner	at the park
in the kitchen	during lunch
out in space	on the road
in the morning	at the pet shop
at one o'clock	at four o'clock
at school	on a train
in winter	at the zoo
in summer	on the ice
beside a ship	during breakfast
late at night	on a snow-covered mountain

205

Appreciating Literature

Critical Thinking

♦ **Directions:** Use your reading skills to answer each riddle. Unscramble the word to check your answer. Write the correct word on the line.

I am a ruler, but I have two feet, not one.

_____

- - - - - - - - - - - - - - - -

I am a _____ .

(ngik)

I am very bright, but that doesn't make me smart.

_____

- - - - - - - - - - - - - - - -

I am the_____ .

(uns)

You can turn me around, but I won't get dizzy.

_____

- - - - - - - - - - - - - - - -

I am a _____ .

(eky)

I can rattle, but I am not a baby's toy.

_____

- - - - - - - - - - - - - - - -

I am a _____ .

(nekas)

I will give you milk, but not in a bottle.

_____

- - - - - - - - - - - - - - - -

I am a _____ .

(ocw)

I smell, but I have no nose.

_____

- - - - - - - - - - - - - - - -

I am a _____ .

(oerflw)

Critical Thinking

Clues About Cats

Name

♦ **Directions:** Read the clues carefully. Then, number the cats. When you are sure you are correct, color the cats.

1. A gray cat sits on the gate.

2. A cat with orange and black spots sits near the tree.

3. A brown cat sits near the bush.

4. A white cat sits between the orange and black spotted cat and the gray cat.

5. A black cat sits next to the brown cat.

6. An orange cat sits between the gray cat and the black cat.

◆ Directions: Cut out the cards. Use your thinking skills to match the picture words with their meanings.

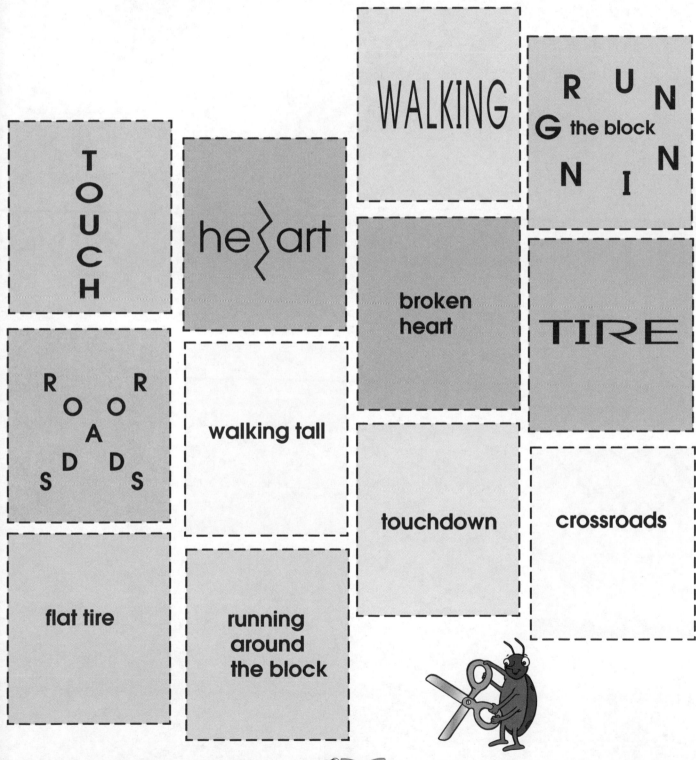

WALKING

R U
G N
the block
N N
I

T
O
U
C
H

he art

broken
heart

R   R
O O
A
D D
S S

TIRE

walking tall

touchdown

crossroads

flat tire

running
around
the block

209

REMARKABLE READER

Award

Awarded to

_____
Name

on _____
Date

**for great
reading comprehension work**

in the
Complete Book of Reading
Grades 1 and 2

ABC Dots

Name

♦ **Directions:** Connect the dots. Begin with **A**. Follow the letters of the alphabet.

214

What Comes First?

Name _____

The first letter of each word is used to put words in alphabetical (ABC) order.

Example: <u>a</u>pple   <u>b</u>ee   <u>c</u>ar

◆ **Directions:** Underline the first letter of each word. Then, write the words in alphabetical order.

<u>a</u>pple
<u>b</u>ee
<u>c</u>ar

---

sun    baby

1. _____

2. _____

nest    hen

1. _____

2. _____

jar   dog

1. _____

2. _____

girl   key

1. _____

2. _____

       Alphabetical Order

Planting an ABC Garden

♦ **Directions:** Help Mr. Murphy plant his vegetables in ABC order. Read the names of the vegetables in the word box. Write the names in the correct rows.

| corn | lettuce | potatoes |
| onions | asparagus | radishes |

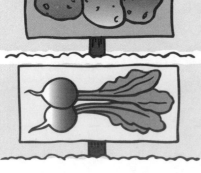

216

What's My Name?

Name

Different words have different jobs. A naming word names a person, place or thing. Naming words are also called **nouns**.

Example: person — nurse
place — store
thing — drum

♦ **Directions:** In the word box below, circle only the words that name a person, place or thing. Then, use the nouns you circled to name each picture.

teacher	up	dog	the	library
runs	is	cowhand	cap	zoo

_____
_____
_____

_____
_____
_____

_____
_____
_____

_____
_____
_____

_____
_____
_____

_____
_____
_____

Nouns

Person, Place or Thing?

Name

◆ **Directions:** Write each noun in the correct box below.

girl	park	truck	vase
artist	tree	doctor	zoo
school	store	ball	baby

Person

Place

Thing

Finding Nouns

Name _____

A noun names a person, place or thing.

♦ **Directions:** Circle two nouns in each sentence below.

The (pig) has a curly (tail).

The hen is sitting on her nest.

A horse is in the barn.

The goat has horns.

The cow has a calf.

The farmer is painting the fence.

Nouns

Nouns at Play

♦ **Directions:** Complete each sentence with the correct noun from
the word box. Write the noun on the line.

ducks	boys
dog	tree
sun	bird

1. A big _____ grows in the park.

2. The _____ is in the sky.

3. A _____ digs a hole.

4. Three _____ swim in the water.

5. A _____ sits on its nest.

6. Two _____ fly a kite.

220

Proper Nouns

Some nouns are special. They name particular persons, places and things. They are called **proper nouns**. Proper nouns always begin with capital letters.

Example: person — Gina
place — Main Street
thing — Golden Gate Bridge

♦ **Directions:** Fill in the circle beside the sentence that is written correctly.

○ Jason calls his dog Ben.
○ Jason calls his dog ben.

○ My friend comes from china.
○ My friend comes from China.

○ The winner is a horse named lucky.
○ The winner is a horse named Lucky.

○ Beth gave Mrs. Jackson an apple.
○ Beth gave mrs. jackson an apple.

Nouns

One or More Than One?

◆ **Directions:** Circle the correct word under each picture.

hat   (hats)

car   cars

frog   frogs

shirt   shirts

cloud   clouds

wheel   wheels

dish   dishes

glass   glasses

fox   foxes

How Many Toys?

Name

♦ **Directions:** Read the nouns under the pictures. Write each noun under **One** or **More Than One**.

yo-yos

boat

jet

doll

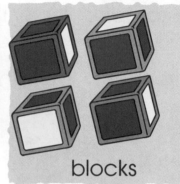
blocks

cars

drum

balls

One	**More Than One**

Nouns

Making Nouns Plural

A **plural noun** means more than one. Add **s** to most nouns to make plural nouns.

Example: Penny has one **dog**.
Jerry has two **dogs**.

♦ **Directions:** Write the plural form of the nouns below.

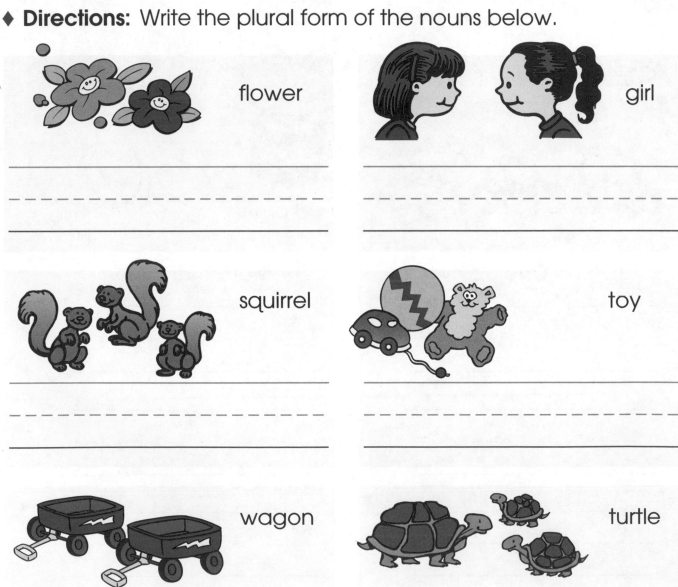

flower

girl

squirrel

toy

wagon

turtle

One Is Not Enough!

A plural noun means more than one. To make nouns that end in **x**, **s**, **ss**, **sh** or **ch** plural, add **es**.

    Example: Barry filled one **box** with sand.
                 Barry filled four **boxes** with sand.

♦ **Directions:** Write the plural form of each noun below.

peach

brush

fox

dress

bus

witch

Nouns

Use the Clues

♦ **Directions:** Write each word from the word box in the correct place. Remember that plural forms usually end in **s**.

kites   star   chick   foxes   matches   lunch

One

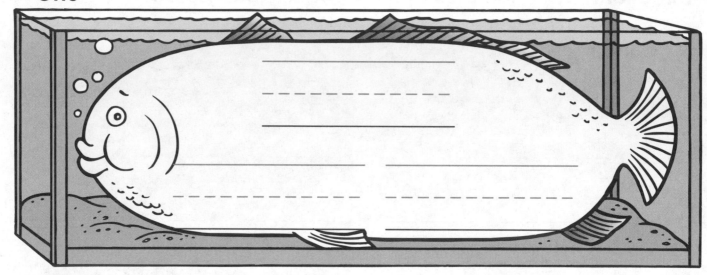

More Than One (Plural)

Name

An **action word** tells what a person or thing can do.

   Example: Fred **kicks** the ball.

♦ **Directions:** Read the words below. Circle words that tell what the children are doing.

jump
boy

sleep
bed

hello
talk

skate
mittens

hop
sidewalk

sing
song

swim
deep

story
read

Verbs

Action Words

♦ **Directions:** Underline the action word in each sentence. Then, draw a line to match each sentence with the correct picture.

The dog <u>barks</u>.

The birds fly.

A fish swims.

A monkey swings.

A turtle crawls.

A boy talks.

Verbs

228

What Is a Verb?

A **verb** is an action word. A verb tells what a person or thing does.

Example: Jane **reads** a book.

◆ **Directions:** Circle the verb in each sentence below.

Two tiny dogs dance.

The bear climbs a ladder.

The clown falls down.

A tiger jumps through a ring.

A boy eats popcorn.

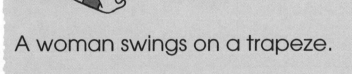

A woman swings on a trapeze.

Verbs

Verbs With One

Name _____

Some verbs tell what one person or thing does. Most of those verbs end in **s**.

Example: Boys **like** pets.
One boy **likes** pets.

♦ **Directions:** Add **s** to each verb to make it tell about one. Write the verb.

Many fish swim. One fish _____.

Snakes glide. One snake _____.

Rabbits hop. One rabbit _____.

Dogs bark. One dog _____.

Birds sing. One bird _____.

Verbs

230

Using Is, Are and Am

The words **is**, **are** and **am** are special verbs.

Use **is** to tell about one person or thing.
Use **are** to tell about more than one.

Use **are** with the word **you**. Use **am** with the word **I**.

♦ **Directions:** Write **is**, **are** or **am** in each sentence below.

The lake _____ deep.

Many fish _____ under the water.

I _____ at the lake.

Sally _____ with me.

We _____ busy catching fish.

You _____ welcome to join us.

231

Verbs

Now or in the Past

A verb can tell about something that happened in the past. For most verbs, add **ed** to tell about the past.

Example: Today, Tara and Jim **walk** to school.
Yesterday, Tara and Jim **walked** to school.

♦ **Directions:** Write the correct verb in each sentence.

follow, followed
_____

- - - - - - - - - - - - - - - - - - - -

Two weeks ago, a puppy _____ me home.

seems, seemed
_____

- - - - - - - - - - - - - - - - - - - -

The puppy _____ hungry.

look, looked
_____

- - - - - - - - - - - - - - - - - - - -

Last week, we _____ for its owner.

play, played
_____

- - - - - - - - - - - - - - - - - - - -

Now, the puppy and I _____ every day.

waits, waited
_____

- - - - - - - - - - - - - - -

She _____ at home for me when I am at school.

Doubling Final Consonants

Most verbs add **ed** to tell about the past. For verbs that end in a single consonant, double the consonant before adding **ed**.

Example: Bunnies **hop** into the garden.
Bunnies **hopped** into the garden.

♦ **Directions:** In each sentence, circle the verb spelled correctly.

The boy ___ peted / petted ___ the dog.

In our game, I ___ tagged / taged ___ you.

My chair ___ tipped / tiped ___ over.

Your kitten ___ rubed / rubbed ___ against my leg.

The men ___ jogged / joged ___ down the street.

Verbs

Writing About the Past

Most verbs add **ed** to tell about the past.

For verbs that end in a silent **e**, drop the **e** before adding **ed**.

For verbs that end in a consonant and **y**, change the **y** to **i** before adding **ed**.

Example: Today, we **like** planes.
Planes **carry** us far.
Long ago, people **liked** horses.
Horses **carried** them far.

♦ **Directions:** In which sentence is the verb spelled correctly?
Fill in the circle beside that sentence.

○ For many years, people tryed to fly.
○ For many years, people tried to fly.

○ Some people moveed their arms up and down quickly.
○ Some people moved their arms up and down quickly.

○ Others hoped for magic carpets.
○ Others hopeed for magic carpets.

○ At last, an airplane staied in the air.
○ At last, an airplane stayed in the air.

○ Later, builders copied the first plane.
○ Later, builders copyed the first plane.

Verbs

Verbs That Change

Some verbs change in special ways to tell about the past. Here are a few important verbs that change in special ways.

♦ **Directions:** In each sentence, write a verb from the box to tell about the past.

Now	Past	Now	Past
come	came	make	made
eat	ate	run	ran
have, has	had	write	wrote

My grandmother _____ me a letter.

At lunch yesterday, I _____ an orange.

Last week, we _____ home from a trip.

This morning, we _____ in a race.

Last winter, I _____ some blue gloves, but now I have red ones.

Verbs

Using Was and Were

Use **was** and **were** to tell about the past. Use **was** to tell about one person or thing. Use **were** to tell about more than one person or thing. Always use **were** with the word **you**.

♦ **Directions:** Write **was** or **were** in each sentence below.

Lois _____ in the second grade last year.

She _____ eight years old.

Carmen and Judy _____ friends.

They _____ on the same soccer team.

I _____ on the team, too.

You _____ too young to play.

Verbs

236

Using the Verb Give

Use **give** and **gives** to tell about now.
Use **gave** to tell about the past.

♦ **Directions:** Write **give**, **gives** or
gave in each
sentence below.

Trisha _____ a party last week.

Bananas _____ me a rash.

I _____ my dog some water every day.

Jill _____ the jacket to me yesterday.

The teacher always _____ a test on Friday.

She _____ Mike a turn as line leader yesterday.

Verbs

Contraction Action

You can combine two words to make one new word. If you leave out a letter and add the mark **'** in its place, you make a **contraction**. To make some contractions, combine a verb and the word **not**.

Example: is + not = isn̶o̶t = isn't

♦ **Directions:** Match these verbs and the word **not** with the contractions.

does + not   haven't

should + not   isn't

is + not   doesn't

have + not   shouldn't

♦ **Directions:** Choose the contraction for the underlined words. Fill in the circle beside the correct contraction.

The baby <u>could not</u> see his sister.

    ◯ couldn't

    ◯ can't

He <u>was not</u> worried, though.

    ◯ hasn't

    ◯ wasn't

She <u>would not</u> go away for long.

    ◯ doesn't

    ◯ wouldn't

Verbs

Words That Describe

Name

Some words describe a person, place or thing. These words tell more about a naming word.

Example: The shoe is **old**.

♦ **Directions:** Read these words that describe. Write the correct word under each picture.

cold	round	funny
light	sad	fat

Describe It!

♦ **Directions:** Match the describing word with the correct picture.

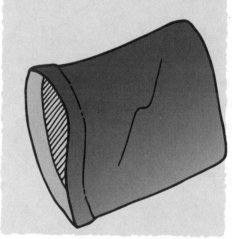

old

soft

hot

sweet

wet

tall

Adjectives

 240

Tell Me More!

A **describing word** tells about a noun. It can tell what kind, what color, what size, what shape or how many.

♦ **Directions:** Write a describing word in each sentence below. Use the words in the box.

green	big	three	round	bushy	six

A _____ has _____ teeth.

A _____ has a _____ tail.

A _____ has _____ legs.

The _____ will become a _____ frog.

The _____ hang by their tails.

An _____ has _____ eyes.

241

Adjectives

What Is It Like?

Name

Describing words tell about persons, places and things. They can tell how things look, taste, sound or feel.

♦ **Directions:** Circle two describing words in each sentence below.

The white kitten is fluffy.

Noisy squirrels ran up a tall tree.

The old book is torn.

The apple was sweet and crisp.

The bright sun is warm.

Yellow ducks swam in a little pond.

Adjectives

242

What Color Is It?

Name _____

Color words are describing words.

Example: Sue has a **blue** dress.
The banana is **yellow**.

♦ **Directions:** Underline the color words in these sentences. Use these describing words to help you color the picture.

1. The leaves on the tree are green.

2. The tree has red apples.

3. A brown squirrel sits by the tree.

4. The house is blue.

5. Purple flowers grow in the yard.

6. Yellow birds fly in the sky.

Adjectives

Weather Words

Weather words are describing words. They tell what kind.

sunny

cloudy

rainy

snowy

windy

♦ **Directions:** Write the correct weather word on the line in each sentence.

We can build a on a _____ day.

You need an on a _____ day.

Your may blow off on a _____ day.

You may wear on a _____ day.

We may not see the ☀ on a _____ day.

How Many Do You See?

Name _____

Number words are describing words. They tell how many.

Example: Two ants crawled across the table.

♦ **Directions:** Read the sentences below. In each sentence, underline the describing word that tells how many. Then, look at the picture. Write an **X** after the sentence that uses an incorrect number word.

1. Four spiders hung in the doorway.

2. The witch held three apples.

3. In the window were two jack-o'-lanterns.

4. One cat sat under the table.

5. Eight bats hung upside down.

Adjectives

Fish for Describing Words

◆ **Directions:** Color only the fish with describing words.

rug

sunny

loud

green

good

big

warm

bed

quilt

moan

old

hot

Adjectives

246

Telling the Whole Story

Name _____

A **sentence** tells a whole idea.

◆ **Directions:** Read each sentence. Write the number by the correct picture. Color the pictures.

1. A bee is on the flower.

2. Two ducks are in the pond.

3. Big clouds are in the sky.

4. The boy has a new kite.

5. A bird sits in the tree.

247

Identifying Sentences

Choosing Sentences

Name

A sentence must tell a whole idea.

♦ **Directions:** Read each group of words. Color the airplane red if the words make a sentence. Color the airplane blue if the words do not make a sentence.

Today is sunny and warm.

The drummer in the band

My friends play ball after school.

The room was full of toys.

The old house seems

My birthday cake is yummy.

♦ **Directions:** Answer the question. _ _ _ _ _ _ _ _ _

How many sentences do you have? _____

248

Writing Sentences Right

A sentence always begins with a capital letter.

Example: **T**he sun is shining.

♦ **Directions:** Write each sentence correctly.

the wind is strong.

_____

- - - - - - - - - - - - - - - - - -

_____

we made a snowman.

_____

- - - - - - - - - - - - - - - - - -

_____

puddles are fun.

_____

- - - - - - - - - - - - - - - - - -

_____

leaves fell all day.

_____

- - - - - - - - - - - - - - - - - -

_____

Identifying Sentences

A Big Finish

Every sentence ends with one of these end marks.

.   ?   !

◆ **Directions:** Fill in the circle beside the sentence that is
written correctly.

○ Terry has new skates.
○ Terry has new skates

○ Watch her zoom
○ Watch her zoom!

○ Does she wear pads on her knees?
○ Does she wear pads on her knees

○ Wear a helmet when you skate
○ Wear a helmet when you skate.

○ Skating is fun!
○ Skating is fun

Identifying Sentences   250   © 2001 McGraw Hill Education. All Rights Reserved.

Sentence Building Blocks

Every sentence has two parts. The **naming part** tells who or what is doing something. The **action part** tells what the person or thing does.

♦ **Directions:** Match each naming part with an action part that makes sense.

Naming part	Action part

My sister ----- has wings.

That bird likes ice cream.

The little boy   cluck.

The goat   takes a picture.

The hens   eats grass.

Mom   walks by the cart.

Mike   rides in the cart.

Little Amy   pushes the cart.

        Parts of a Sentence

Completing Sentences

♦ **Directions:** Each sentence is missing either a naming part or an action part. Fill in the circle beside the group of words that forms the missing part.

My neighbor _____

○ is having a yard sale today.   ○ in the house next door.

One man _____

○ at the sale.   ○ likes old books.

_____ look for old toys.

○ Many people   ○ In the morning

_____ wants an old checkers game.

○ By the door   ○ My brother

Two ladies _____

○ buy an old toy chest.   ○ a teddy bear.

Finding Naming Parts

Name _____

The naming part of a sentence tells who or what is doing something.

Example: The **chimp on a bike** rode in a circle.

♦ **Directions:** Underline the naming part in each sentence below.

1. Our class had a picnic in the park.

2. Some teachers played ball with us.

3. The hotdogs were tasty.

4. Big oak trees grew along a road.

5. A man in tennis shoes ran in a race.

6. A woman fished all morning.

253

Parts of a Sentence

Writing Naming Parts

♦ **Directions:** Read the naming parts in the tent. Write one of the naming parts to begin each sentence.

Rain

Black clouds

A big wind

Todd and Clint

The old tent

1. _____went camping.

2. _____ was hard to set up.

3. _____ blew the trees.

4. _____ filled the sky.

5. _____ fell on the tent.

  254

Action at the Zoo

The action part of a sentence tells what the naming part is doing or did.

Example: The zookeeper **opened the gate**.

♦ **Directions:** Underline the action part in each sentence below.

1. My family walked to the zoo.

2. The seals swam in a pool of water.

3. A monkey climbed a tree.

4. Two big elephants swung their trunks.

5. A striped tiger paced in its cage.

6. The giraffe stretched its long neck.

255

Parts of a Sentence

It's Time for Action!

♦ **Directions:** Write one of these action parts to finish each sentence.

came from the roof
put out the fire
raced to the fire
blew loudly
held a big hose

The firetruck _____ .

The siren _____ .

Flames _____ .

Firefighters _____ .

Water _____ .

256

Circus Sentences

Name

♦ **Directions:** The boxes at the bottom of this page have sentence parts. Some are naming parts. Some are action parts. Cut out all the boxes. Look at each picture. Glue the correct naming part and action part beside each picture. Read each sentence that you make.

Naming Part	Action Part

Naming Part	Action Part

Naming Part	Action Part

Naming Part	Action Part

The bear	go up in the sky.	is barking.
The balloons	wears a costume.	An elephant
	The dog	leads the parade.

257

Parts of a Sentence

Is Anything Missing?

♦ **Directions:** Read each group of words. Is it a complete sentence that tells a whole idea? Is it missing a naming part? Is it missing an action part? Fill in the circle beside the correct answer.

is going to the big game tonight

○ Complete sentence

○ Missing a naming part

○ Missing an action part

The fans cheer for their team.

○ Complete sentence

○ Missing a naming part

○ Missing an action part

Hot dogs

○ Complete sentence

○ Missing a naming part

○ Missing an action part

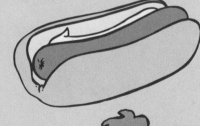

The cheerleaders jump and yell for our team.

○ Complete sentence

○ Missing a naming part

○ Missing an action part

Parts of a Sentence

Sentences That Tell

Some sentences tell something. Every **telling sentence** ends with a **period**.

Example: The bird sings**.**

♦ **Directions:** Circle only the sentences that tell something.

1. Two turtles sat on a log.

2. One turtle fell off.

3. Did you see her?

4. She swam away.

5. The water is cold.

6. Can you swim?

Sentences That Ask

Some sentences ask something. An **asking sentence** is called a **question**. A question ends with a **question mark**.

Example: What is your name**?**

♦ **Directions:** Circle only the questions.

1. Is that your house?

2. There are two pictures on the wall.

3. Where do you sleep?

4. Do you watch TV in that room?

5. Which coat is yours?

6. The kitten is asleep.

Kinds of Sentences

Questions, Questions

A question begins with a capital letter and ends with a question mark.

♦ **Directions:** Write each question correctly on the line.

is our class going to the Science Museum

_____

- -

_____

- -

_____

will we see dinosaur bones

_____

- -

_____

- -

_____

does the museum have a mummy

_____

- -

_____

- -

_____

Kinds of Sentences

Name _____

A telling sentence ends with a period. A question ends with a question mark.

◆ **Directions:** Read each sentence. Put the correct end mark after each sentence.

1. Is winter coming ☐

2. Snow is falling in the woods ☐

3. The trees are covered with snow ☐

4. Is the bear lost ☐

5. The bear is looking for his cave ☐

6. The bear is cold and sleepy ☐

7. Is the bear ready for a long nap ☐

8. Will the bear sleep all winter ☐

263

Kinds of Sentences

Changing Sentences

The order of words can change a sentence.

Example: **Telling sentence:** The girl can jump high.
Asking sentence: Can the girl jump high?

♦ **Directions:** Read each telling sentence. Change the order of the words to make a question. Write your question on the line.

The clown is happy.

_____

- -

_____

The boy can swim.

_____

- -

_____

The bell will ring.

_____

- -

_____

The popcorn is hot.

_____

- -

_____

I'm So Excited!

The end mark **!** shows that you are excited.
Use it to end a sentence that shows strong feelings.

Example: What a beautiful day this is**!**

♦ **Directions:** Read these sentences. Write **?** or **!** after each sentence.

? or !

1. What a great day this is for a race ☐

2. Who is running in this race ☐

3. How fast they run ☐

4. Who will finish first ☐

5. The runners are off ☐

6. Run faster ☐

7. Can you see the finish line ☐

8. I won the race ☐

Kinds of Sentences

Follow My Directions.

You can write orders in sentences. If you are excited, end your order with **!**. If you are not excited, end your order with a period.

Example: Watch out for that hole in the road!
Ride slowly.

♦ **Directions:** Fill in the circle beside the sentence
that is written correctly.

○ Follow these steps to find the treasure.

○ Follow these steps to find the treasure?

○ First, go to the old tree?

○ First, go to the old tree.

○ Watch out for angry bees!

○ Watch out for angry bees?

○ Take five steps toward the big rock?

○ Take five steps toward the big rock.

○ Dig for the treasure. Hurry!

○ Dig for the treasure? Hurry.

○ Look at all my gold and jewels?

○ Look at all my gold and jewels!

Kinds of Sentences

Sentence Combining

Two sentences can become one sentence. Use the word **and** to join them. Leave out words that are repeated.

Example: I have a ball. I have a bat.
I have a ball **and** a bat.

♦ **Directions:** Read the two sentences. Write them as one sentence.

My friend has a cat. My friend has a dog.

_____

My friend has _____ .

I eat with a fork. I eat with a spoon.

_____

I eat with _____ .

Dad needs a rake. Dad needs a basket.

_____

Dad needs _____ .

The rabbit likes carrots. The rabbit likes peas.

_____

The rabbit likes _____ .

Combining Sentences

Using and in Sentences

Two sentences can become one sentence. You can use the word **and** to join them.

Examples: Maria sings. She hums, too.   Maria sings **and** hums.
Maria sings. Sean sings, too. Maria **and** Sean sing.

♦ **Directions:** Read the two sentences. Write them as one sentence.

I read books. I write books, too.

_____

- -

_____

_____

- -

_____

Jim skis. Ida skis, too.

- -

_____

Juan runs. He kicks.

_____

- -

_____

_____

- -

_____

Combining Sentences

Name _____

◆ **Directions:** Read the two sentences. Find the sentence parts below that tell the same idea. Cut out and glue the sentence parts to make one sentence.

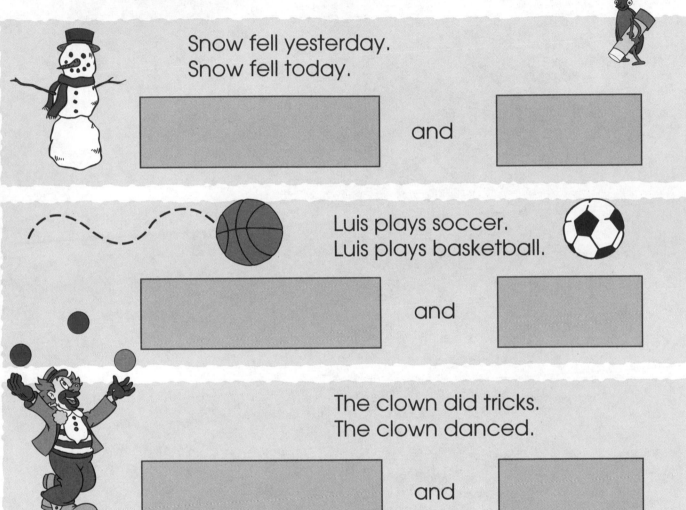

Snow fell yesterday.
Snow fell today.

[   ]   and   [   ]

Luis plays soccer.
Luis plays basketball.

[   ]   and   [   ]

The clown did tricks.
The clown danced.

[   ]   and   [   ]

The clown did tricks	basketball.	Snow fell yesterday
danced.	today.	Luis plays soccer

Pulling It All Together

Name _____

◆ **Directions:** Read the two sentences.
Write them as one sentence.

Birds live in the tree. Squirrels live in the tree.

_____

_____

_____

_____

Dad washed the car. Dad waxed the car.

_____

_____

_____

_____

Mom planted beans. Mom planted corn.

_____

_____

_____

_____

Combining Sentences

A sentence makes sense when the words are in order.

◆ **Directions:** Write the numerals 1, 2, 3 and 4 in the circles to put the words in order. Write the words in the correct order to make a sentence.

painting.   doghouse   needs   The

have   I   paint.   red   Red

happy.   very   is   Spot

Groups of Words

Name

Changing groups of words in a sentence changes the meaning.

Example: The boy is **in the car**.

The boy is **in the water**.

♦ **Directions:** Cut out and glue a word group to complete each sentence. Draw a picture to show the meaning of the sentence. Color the picture.

1. The fish [   ] is yellow.

2. I see a kite [   ] .

3. That box [   ] is yours.

in the bowl	under the tree	of oranges
over the tree	with a smiley face	in the lake

Building Sentences

Word Order

Changing the order of the words in a sentence may change the meaning.

Example: The dog chased the cat.

The cat chased the dog.

♦ **Directions:** Read the sentence pairs. Circle the sentence that goes with the picture.

The boy hit the ball.

The ball hit the boy.

The giant watched the elf.

The elf watched the giant.

The teacher read to the girl.

The girl read to the teacher.

The baby laughed at the father.

The father laughed at the baby.

The frog jumped over the rabbit.

The rabbit jumped over the frog.

Building Sentences

What Kind?

Name _____

Words that describe make a sentence better.

Example: I have a coat.
I have a **red** coat **with many pockets**.

♦ **Directions:** Read each sentence. Write a word from the box on each line to make the sentences more interesting. Draw a picture of each sentence.

bright	strong	little
brave	graceful	precious

The skater won a medal.

_____

The _____ skater won

_____

a _____ medal.

The jewels are in the safe.

_____

The _____ jewels

_____

are in the _____ safe.

How Does It Happen?

Name

A sentence can tell what a person or thing does. It can also tell how, when or where the person or thing does the action.

Example: Ada walked.
Then, Ada walked quickly from the room.

How? quickly

When? Then

Where? from the room

♦ **Directions:** In each sentence, write a word or words to answer the question. If you like, use words from this box.

| noisily | in the show | at night | before lunch | on the stage |
| loudly | around | nearby | in the yard | with energy |

_____

My dog was barking_____ . **How?**

_____

My dog was barking_____ . **When?**

_____

Dave sang _____ . **Where?**

_____

The girls play _____ . **Where?**

_____

They play_____ . **How?**

Building Sentences

A Sentence That Grows

Name _____

A sentence can tell more and more.

♦ **Directions:** Make the underlined sentence grow by writing a word on each line. On another paper, draw a picture of the last sentence.

<u>I see the elephant.</u>

_____

I see the _____ elephant.

_____

I see the _____ elephant

_____

eating _____ .

_____

I see the _____ elephant

_____

eating _____

_____

as he stands by the _____ .

Another Growing Sentence

Name _____

♦ **Directions:** Complete the first sentence. Make it grow by writing a word on each line. On another sheet of paper, draw a picture of the last sentence.

I found my _____ _____ .

I found my _____ in the _____ .

I found my _____ _____ in the

_____

_____ under a

_____ .

Building Sentences

Joining Sentences

You can join sentences to tell more.

Example: Linda went to the store, **and** I met her there.

Linda went to the store, **but** she didn't buy anything.

♦ **Directions:** What can you join to the sentence to make it tell more? Fill in the circle beside the right ending.

It snowed yesterday, and

- ○ my friends and I made a snowman.
- ○ flowers are pretty.

Jerry had a party, but

- ○ some people skate well.
- ○ not everyone could come.

This book is long, but

- ○ carrots are good for you.
- ○ it is not hard.

The baseball game was called off, and

- ○ we like to swim.
- ○ I went home.

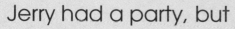

Building Sentences

More on Joining Sentences

You can join sentences to tell more about something.

Example: Julian read a book.
Julian read a book **when** he got home.

♦ **Directions:** Read each sentence. Cut and glue to make the joined sentences tell more.

Tom likes to go to the library.

Tom likes to go to the library | when |

Pete did not do his homework.

Pete did not do his homework | why |

Will you call me?

Will you call me | when |

Tina is saving her money.

Tina is saving her money | why |

as soon as you can? | because she wants a bike.
because he was sick. | when he has free time.

Building Sentences

Adding Why

You can make sentences that tell more. You can add why something happened.

♦ **Directions:** Read the beginning of each sentence. Complete each sentence by telling why something happened.

There was no school yesterday **because** _____

_____

_____

Jerry had a party **because** _____

_____

_____

I am leaving now **because** _____

_____

_____

Building Sentences

Telling a Story in Order

Tell the events of a story in the order they happened. Use the words **first**, **next** and **last** to make the order clear.

♦ **Directions:** The three pictures tell a story. The sentences should tell the same story. Read the given sentence. Then, write two sentences to complete the story.

First: _____

_____

_____

Next: Kim took the bird to a vet who helped it.

_____

Last: _____

_____

_____

284

What Happened Next?

Sentences can tell about events in the order they happened.

♦ **Directions:** Read the sentence. Write two sentences to tell what two things could happen next. Draw a picture to match an event in your story.

Sally went to the shelter to choose a new pet.

_____

_____

_____

_____

_____

_____

_____

_____

Order of Events

Using Sentences in Order

Name

Sentences can tell events in a story in order.

◆ **Directions:** Write 1, 2 and 3 in the circles to tell what happened to Harry first, second and third. Then, write a sentence to tell about each picture. You can use the words from the box in your sentences if you need them.

boat
catch
caught
fight
fish
fought
pole
proud

286

What Did You Say?

Name _____

A sentence can tell what someone is saying.

♦ **Directions:** Look at each picture. Write a sentence in the bubble that tells what the person is saying.

287

Writing Sentences

Writing a Letter

Sentences can make a good letter.

♦ **Directions:** Write a letter to a friend on the lines.

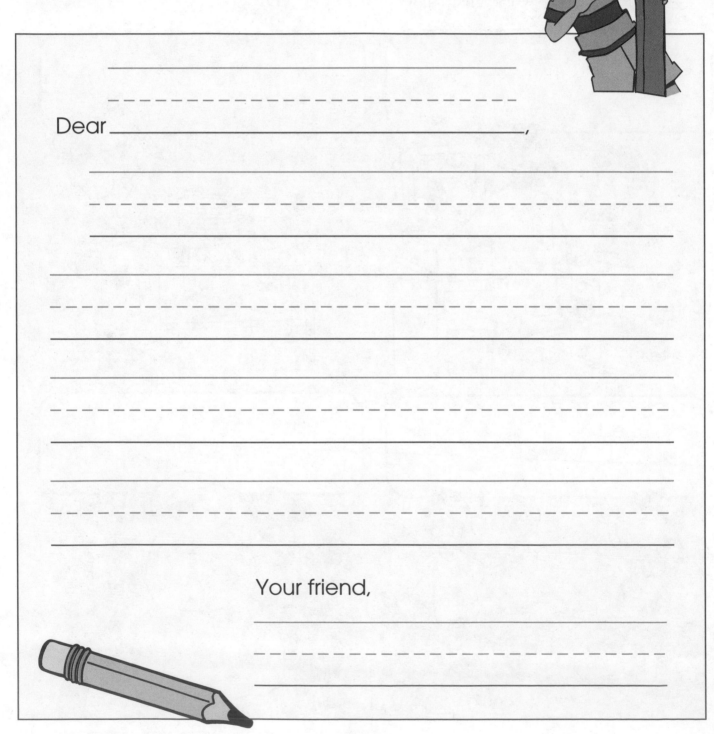

Dear _____,

Your friend,

Writing About the Seasons

Sentences can tell about special times. Every season of the year is special.

♦ **Directions:** Write three words to tell about each season.

Spring

_____

_____

_____

Summer

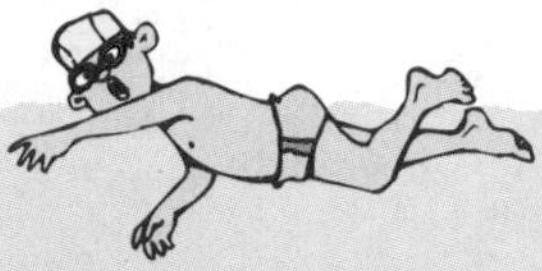

_____

_____

_____

Fall

_____

_____

_____

Winter

_____

_____

_____

Writing Sentences

Let's Take a Trip!

Sentences can tell about special happenings.

◆ **Directions:** Imagine you are going somewhere far away. On the short lines in and around the plane, write words about your trip. Then, use some of the words to write three sentences about the trip.

Brainstorming

Brainstorming is a way to think of new ideas. You can use these ideas in your writing.

◆ **Directions:** Answer the questions below. Use the answers to help you write four sentences about your family.

My Family

How many people are in your family? _____

_____

What are their names? _____

_____

_____

Write two words that tell about each person.

_____

_____

_____

What is your family's favorite meal? _____

_____

What is your family's favorite TV show? _____

Writing Sentences

All About Me

◆ **Directions:** Write sentences to tell about yourself.

_____

- -

_____

- -

_____

- -

Draw yourself.

_____

- -

_____

- -

_____

- -

_____

- -

_____

Writing Sentences

Toad or Frog

Write a book about a toad or a frog! It can be a story that you make up or a report on facts. Follow these steps.

A. Choose an idea. This list may help you.

Story starters	Report ideas
• A frog and a toad's conversation	• A report on a frog
• One day, Mr. Toad hopped into my wagon . . .	• A report on a toad
• *Fred Frog Meets the President*	• From tadpole to frog
• *Ted Toad's Terrific Tree House*	• How to catch a frog

B. Think up your story or do research for your report. Write your story or report on sheets of writing paper. Here are some words you may need.

brown	croak	fly	frog	green
hop	jump	land	legs	lily pad
pond	tadpole	toad	tongue	water

C. Use two sheets of construction paper for the front and back covers of your book. Color the picture on page 297. Cut it out and glue it on your cover.

Make Your Own Storybooks

Sand Castle

Write a book about summer or swimming! You might write about something you have done during summer or your feelings about the season. Follow these steps.

A. Choose an idea. This list may help you.

- *A Day at the Beach*

- *Summer Fun*

- My sand castle looks like . . .

- I love summer because . . .

- While swimming in the lake, I . . .

- I live in a sand castle . . .

- A poem about a sand castle or a day at the beach

- A poem about how summer makes me feel

B. Think up your story. Write your story on sheets of writing paper. Here are some words you may need.

beach	bucket	burn	fish	float
hot	paddle	pail	raft	sand
shells	shore	shovel	sun	sunglasses
swim	swimsuit	tan	towel	water

C. Use two sheets of construction paper for the front and back covers of your book. Color the illustration on page 299. Cut it out and glue it on your cover.

School Bus

Write a book about a real school bus or an imaginary one. You can tell about somewhere you have gone on a bus or somewhere you wish you could go. Follow these steps.

A. Choose an idea. This list may help you.

- I was riding the school bus when suddenly . . .

- Oh no! I got on the wrong bus . . .

- Write a poem about a trip on a school bus.

- *The Magical Mystery Bus*

- Write a story about what it would be like to be a bus driver.

- The school bus takes us to many great places . . .

B. Think up your story. Write your story on sheets of writing paper. Here are some words you may need.

backpack	boys	bus	children	driver
feet	friends	girls	homework	lunch
run	school	sing	stop	street
students	talk	teacher	walk	yellow

C. Use two sheets of construction paper for the front and back covers of your book. Color the illustration on page 301. Cut it out and glue it on your cover.

Make Your Own Storybooks

Out in Space

You can write a book about space! You can report facts about space or make up a story about adventures in space. Follow these steps.

A. Choose an idea. This list may help you.

Story starters	**Report ideas**

Story starters

- Walking on the moon, we came face to face with . . .

- While on the space shuttle . . .

- *Our Vacation on Planet _____*

- *The Friendly Alien*

Report ideas

- *Space Station for the Future*

- *All About the Planet Mercury* (or another planet)

- To become an astronaut, I would . . .

- *Humans in Space*

B. Think up your story or do research for your report. Write your story or report on sheets of writing paper. Here are some words you may need.

alien	astronaut	camera	comet	craters
fly	land	meteor	moon	orbit
pictures	planets	repair	rocky	satellite
space	spacecraft	space station	space suit	stars
surface	Mercury	Venus	Earth	Mars
Jupiter	Saturn	Uranus	Neptune	Pluto

C. Use two sheets of construction paper for the front and back covers of your book. Color the picture on page 303. Cut it out and glue it on your cover.

Make Your Own Storybooks

296

Toad Pattern

Make Your Own Storybooks

Sand Castle Pattern

Make Your Own Storybooks

School Bus Pattern

Name _____

301

Make Your Own Storybooks

Out in Space Pattern

Name _____

Make Your Own Storybooks

BLUE RIBBON
WRITER
Award

Awarded to

_____
Name

on _____
Date

for great
grammar and writing work

in the
Complete Book of Reading
Grades 1 and 2

Color the Letter Partners

Letter partners are capital and small letters that go together. These pairs of letters are letter partners: Aa, Bb, Cc, Dd, Ee, Ff, Gg, Hh, Ii, Jj, Kk, Ll, Mm, Nn, Oo, Pp, Qq, Rr, Ss, Tt, Uu, Vv, Ww, Xx, Yy, Zz.

♦ **Directions:** Use a different color to color each pair of letter partners.

Letter Recognition

6

Partner Match

♦ **Directions:** Draw a line from each letter in the beehive to its partner letter.

Letter Recognition

7

Partner Search

♦ **Directions:** Color fish with letter partners yellow. Color the other fish blue. Follow the yellow path to the island.

Letter Recognition

8

Sounds the Same

Different words may begin with the same sound.

Example: **Box** and **boy** begin with the same sound. **Cat** and **dog** do not.

♦ **Directions:** Say each picture's name. Color the pictures in the box if their names begin with the same sound.

Auditory Discrimination

9

Tic-Tac-Toe

♦ **Directions:** Find the three pictures in each game whose names begin with the same sound. Draw a line through them.

Auditory Discrimination

10

Answer Key

Read and Rhyme

Words that end with the same sounds are words that rhyme.

Hot and **pot** rhyme.
Hot and **pup** do not rhyme.

♦ **Directions:** Cut out the pictures at the bottom of the page. Say the name of each picture. In each row, glue the pictures whose names rhyme.

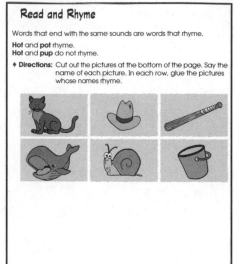

Auditory Discrimination

11

Write and Hear Mm

M and **m** are letter partners.
Map begins with the sound of **Mm**.

♦ **Directions:** Trace the letter. Write it on the line.

M M M M M

m m m m m m

♦ **Directions:** Color the pictures whose names begin with the sound of **m**.

Initial Consonant Mm

13

Write and Hear Ss

S and **s** are letter partners.
Sock begins with the sound of **Ss**.

♦ **Directions:** Trace the letter. Write it on the line.

S S S S S S S

s s s s s s s s s s s

♦ **Directions:** Circle the socks with pictures whose names begin with the sound of **s**.

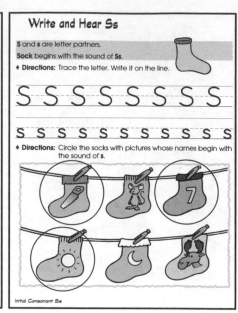

Initial Consonant Ss

14

Write and Hear Tt

T and **t** are letter partners.
Tiger begins with the sound of **Tt**.

♦ **Directions:** Trace the letter. Write it on the line.

T T T T T T T T

t t t t t t t t t t t

♦ **Directions:** Color the pictures whose names begin with the sound of **t**.

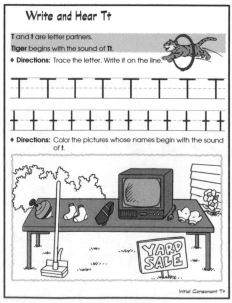

Initial Consonant Tt

15

Write and Hear Hh

H and **h** are letter partners.
Hat begins with the sound of **Hh**.

♦ **Directions:** Trace the letter. Write it on the line.

H H H H H H H

h h h h h h h h h h h

♦ **Directions:** Play Tic-Tac-Toe. Find three pictures in a row whose names begin with the sound of **h**. Draw a line through them.

Initial Consonant Hh

16

Write and Hear Kk

K and **k** are letter partners.
Kitten begins with the sound of **Kk**.

♦ **Directions:** Trace the letter. Write it on the line.

K K K K K K K K

k k k k k k k k k k k

♦ **Directions:** Color the pictures whose names begin with the sound of **k**.

Initial Consonant Kk

17

Answer Key

308

ABCDEFGHIJKL

Write and Hear Bb

B and **b** are letter partners.
Ball begins with the sound of **Bb**.

♦ **Directions:** Trace the letter. Write it on the line.

B B B B B B B B B

b b b b b b b b b

♦ **Directions:** Color the bow if the name of the picture on the box begins with the sound of **b**.

18

19

Write and Hear Ff

F and **f** are letter partners.
Fox begins with the sound of **Ff**.

♦ **Directions:** Trace the letter. Write it on the line.

F F F F F F F F F

f f f f f f f f f f

♦ **Directions:** Help the farmer find the fox. Draw a line through the pictures whose names begin with the sound of **f**.

Write and Hear Gg

G and **g** are letter partners.
Goat begins with the sound of **Gg**.

♦ **Directions:** Trace the letter. Write it on the line.

G G G G G G G

g g g g g g g g g g g g

♦ **Directions:** Write **g** if the name of the picture begins with the sound of **g**.

20

Write and Hear Ll

L and **l** are letter partners.
Leaf begins with the sound of **Ll**.

♦ **Directions:** Trace the letter. Write it on the line.

L L L L L L L L

l l l l l l l l

♦ **Directions:** Color the leaves with pictures whose names begin with the sound of **l**.

21

Write and Hear Nn

N and **n** are letter partners.
Nest begins with the sound of **Nn**.

♦ **Directions:** Trace the letter. Write it on the line.

N N N N N N N

n n n n n n n n n

♦ **Directions:** Color those pictures whose names begin with the sound of **n**.

22

Answer Key

Write and Hear Dd

D and d are letter partners.
Desk begins with the sound of **Dd**.
♦ **Directions:** Trace the letter. Write it on the line.

D D D D D D D

d d d d d d d d

♦ **Directions:** Color the pictures whose names begin with the sound of **d**.

Initial Consonant Dd

Write and Hear Ww

W and w are letter partners.
Window begins with the sound of **Ww**.
♦ **Directions:** Trace the letter. Write it on the line.

W W W W W

w w w w w w w w

♦ **Directions:** Color the curtains if the name of the picture begins with the sound of **w**.

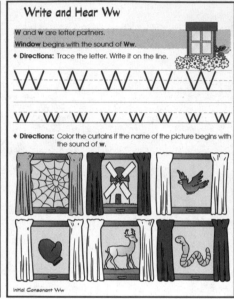

Initial Consonant Ww

Write and Hear Cc

C and c are letter partners.
Cap begins with the sound of **Cc**.
♦ **Directions:** Trace the letter. Write it on the line.

C C C C C C

c c c c c c c c c

♦ **Directions:** Play Tic-Tac-Toe. Find three pictures in a row whose names begin with the sound of **c**. Draw a line through them.

Initial Consonant Cc

23

24

25

Write and Hear Jj

J and j are letter partners.
Jacket begins with the sound of **Jj**.
♦ **Directions:** Trace the letter. Write it on the line.

J J J J J J J

J J J J J J J J

♦ **Directions:** Color the jack-in-the-box if the name of its picture begins with the sound of **j**.

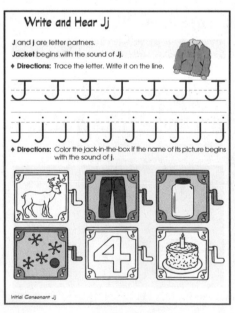

Initial Consonant Jj

Write and Hear Rr

R and r are letter partners.
Ring begins with the sound of **Rr**.
♦ **Directions:** Trace the letter. Write it on the line.

R R R R R R R

r r r r r r r r r r

♦ **Directions:** Write r on the line if the name of the picture begins with the sound of **r**.

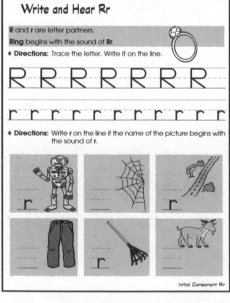

Initial Consonant Rr

Write and Hear Pp

P and p are letter partners.
Pen begins with the sound of **Pp**.
♦ **Directions:** Trace the letter. Write it on the line.

P P P P P P P

p p p p p p p p p

♦ **Directions:** Color the pictures whose names begin with the sound of **p**.

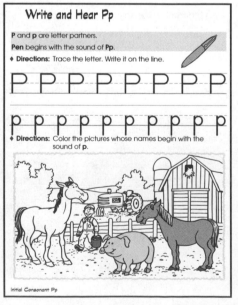

Initial Consonant Pp

26

27

28

Answer Key

310

Write and Hear Vv

V and v are letter partners.
Vase begins with the sound of **Vv**.
♦ **Directions:** Trace the letter. Write it on the line.

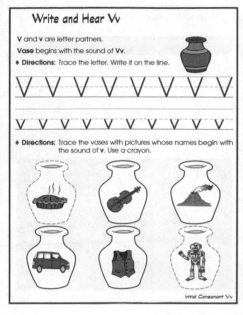

♦ **Directions:** Trace the vases with pictures whose names begin with the sound of **v**. Use a crayon.

Initial Consonant Vv

29

Write and Hear Yy

Y and y are letter partners.
Yellow begins with the sound of **Yy**.
♦ **Directions:** Trace the letter. Write it on the line.

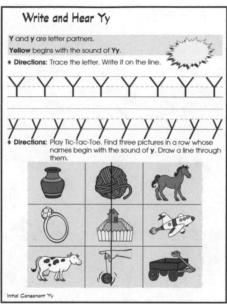

♦ **Directions:** Play Tic-Tac-Toe. Find three pictures in a row whose names begin with the sound of **y**. Draw a line through them.

Initial Consonant Yy

30

Write and Hear Zz

Z and z are letter partners.
Zero begins with the sound of **Zz**.
♦ **Directions:** Trace the letter. Write it on the line.

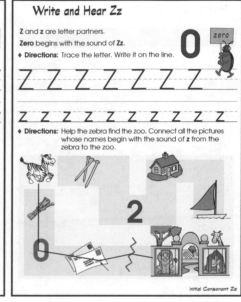

♦ **Directions:** Help the zebra find the zoo. Connect all the pictures whose names begin with the sound of **z** from the zebra to the zoo.

Initial Consonant Zz

31

Write and Hear Qq

Q and q are letter partners.
Queen begins with the sound of **Qq**.
♦ **Directions:** Trace the letter. Write it on the line.

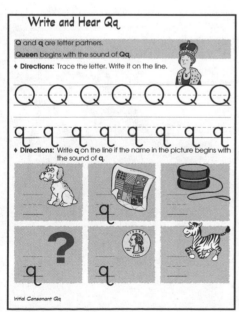

♦ **Directions:** Write **q** on the line if the name in the picture begins with the sound of **q**.

Initial Consonant Qq

32

Match Letters and Sounds

♦ **Directions:** Cut out each letter at the bottom of the page. Find the picture whose name begins with the sound of that letter. Glue the letter in the box beside the picture.

Initial Consonants

33

Write and Hear Xx

X and x are letter partners.
Box ends with the sound of **Xx**.
♦ **Directions:** Trace the letter. Write it on the line.

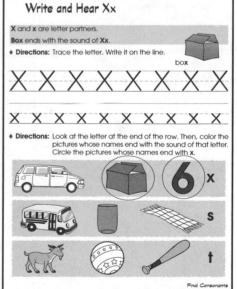

♦ **Directions:** Look at the letter at the end of the row. Then, color the pictures whose names end with the sound of that letter. Circle the pictures whose names end with **x**.

Final Consonants

35

Answer Key

How Does It End?

♦ **Directions:** Write a letter from the box to complete each word.

m k b n p r l d g

drum star bed

tail bib log

fan mop book

Final Consonants

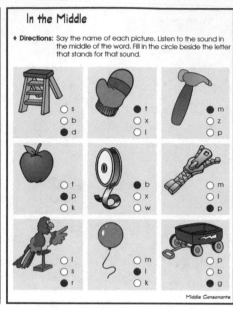

In the Middle

♦ **Directions:** Say the name of each picture. Listen to the sound in the middle of the word. Fill in the circle beside the letter that stands for that sound.

- s
- b
- ● d

- ● t
- x
- l

- ● m
- z
- p

- t
- ● p
- k

- ● b
- x
- w

- m
- l
- ● p

- l
- s
- ● r

- m
- ● l
- k

- p
- b
- ● g

Middle Consonants

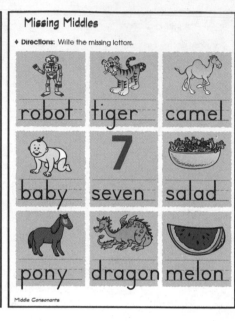

Missing Middles

♦ **Directions:** Write the missing letters.

robot tiger camel

baby seven salad

pony dragon melon

Middle Consonants

Consonant Review

♦ **Directions:** One letter is missing in each word. Write the missing letter on the line.

dog box sun

hen tulip top

log leaf wagon

Consonants in All Positions

Consonant Review

♦ **Directions:** Write all the missing consonants.

man fox pig

bed jar camel

goat van cap

Consonants in All Positions

Answer Key

312

Meet Short a

Listen for the sound of short **a** in **van**.

♦ **Directions:** Trace the letter. Write it on the line.

van

A A A A A A A A A

a a a a a a a a a a a

♦ **Directions:** Color the pictures whose names have the short **a** sound.

Short Vowel a

41

Short a Maze

♦ **Directions:** Help the cat get to the bag. Connect all the pictures whose names have the short **a** sound from the cat to the bag.

Short Vowel a

42

Short a Picture Match

♦ **Directions:** Cut out the cards. Read the words. Match the words and the pictures.

| hat | van | bat | ham |
| bag | man | map | fan |

Short Vowel a

43

Meet Short i

Listen for the sound of short **i** in **pig**.

♦ **Directions:** Trace the letter. Write it on the line.

pig

I I I I I I I I I

i i i i i i i i i

♦ **Directions:** Say the name of each picture. Color the trim on the bib if the name has the short **i** sound.

Short Vowel i

45

Read and Color Short i

♦ **Directions:** Say the name of each picture. Color the pictures whose names have the short **i** sound. The words in the box will give you hints.

| milk | crib | bib |
| pig | kitten | fish |

Short Vowel i

46

The Donkey's Tail

♦ **Directions:** Find the donkey tails with pictures whose names have the short **i** sound. Cut them out. Glue those tails onto the donkeys.

Short Vowel i

47

313

Answer Key

Meet Short u

Listen for the sound of short **u** in **bug**.

♦ **Directions:** Trace the letter.
Write it on the line.

bug

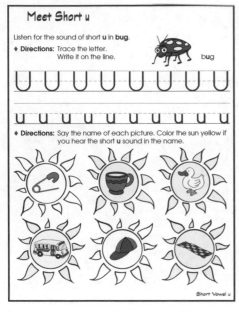

♦ **Directions:** Say the name of each picture. Color the sun yellow if you hear the short **u** sound in the name.

Short Vowel u

49

Short u Tic-Tac-Toe

u

♦ **Directions:** Color the pictures whose names have the short **u** sound. Then, play Tic-Tac-Toe. Draw a line through three colored pictures in a row.

Short Vowel u

50

Feed the Pup

♦ **Directions:** Cut out the picture cards. Say the name of each picture. If the name has the sound of short **u**, glue the card in the pup's bowl.

Short Vowel u

51

Meet Short o

Listen for the sound of short **o** in **fox**.

♦ **Directions:** Trace the letter.
Write it on the line.

fox

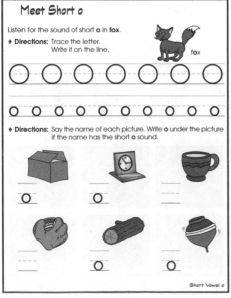

♦ **Directions:** Say the name of each picture. Write **o** under the picture if the name has the short **o** sound.

Short Vowel o

53

Find Short o Words

♦ **Directions:** Underline the pictures whose names have the short **o** sound.

♦ **Directions:** The words that match the underlined pictures above are hidden in this puzzle. Circle the words. They may go **across** or **down**.

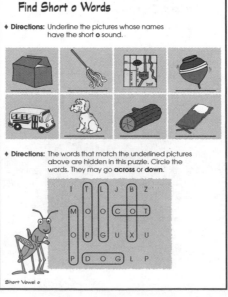

Short Vowel o

54

Short o Puzzles

♦ **Directions:** Cut out the puzzle pieces. Match each picture with its name.

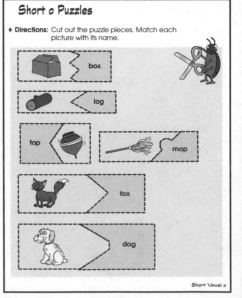

box

log

top

mop

fox

dog

Short Vowel o

55

Answer Key

314

Meet Short e

Listen for the sound of short **e** in **hen**.

♦ **Directions:** Trace the letter.
Write it on the line.

hen

E E E E E E E E E

e e e e e e e e e e

♦ **Directions:** Color the pictures whose names have the short **e** sound.

Short Vowel e

57

A Matching Game

♦ **Directions:** Draw a line to connect each picture with its matching short **e** word.

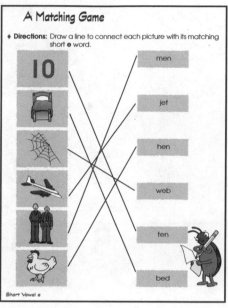

men

jet

hen

web

ten

bed

Short Vowel e

58

Finish-the-Word Puzzles

♦ **Directions:** Write a vowel in the middle of each puzzle that will make a word across and down.

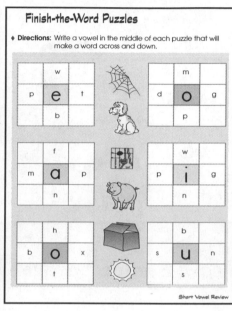

w / p e t / b

m a p / n — f

d o g / p — m

p i g / n — w

h / b o x / t

s u n / s — b

Short Vowel Review

61

Name the Short Vowel

♦ **Directions:** Say the name of the picture. Listen for the short vowel sound. Then, fill in the correct circle.

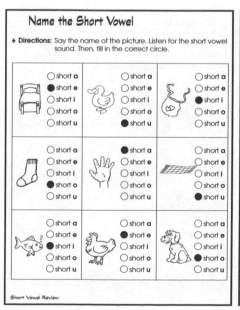

Short Vowel Review

62

Meet Long a

Listen for the sound of long **a** in **cake**.

♦ **Directions:** Color the pictures whose names have the long **a** sound.

cake

Long Vowel a

63

Answer Key

Write Long a

The letters **a__e** usually stand for the long **a** sound.

♦ **Directions:** Write the missing vowels.

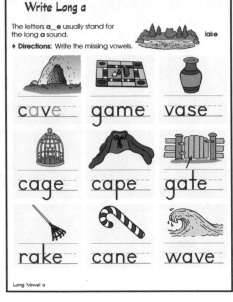

lake

cave　game　vase

cage　cape　gate

rake　cane　wave

Long Vowel a

64

Meet Long i

Listen for the sound of long **i** in **bike**.
Look for **i__e**.

♦ **Directions:** Fill in the circle beside the name of the picture.

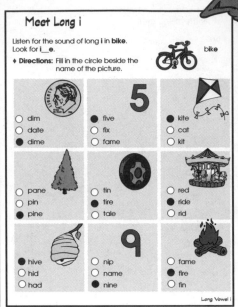

bike

- ○ dim
- ○ date
- ● dime

- ● five
- ○ fix
- ○ fame

- ● kite
- ○ cat
- ○ kit

- ○ pane
- ○ pin
- ● pine

- ● tin
- ● tire
- ○ tale

- ● red
- ● ride
- ○ rid

- ● hive
- ○ hid
- ○ had

- ○ nip
- ○ name
- ● nine

- ● fame
- ● fire
- ○ fin

Long Vowel i

65

Long i and Short i

♦ **Directions:** Write the name of the picture on the correct line.

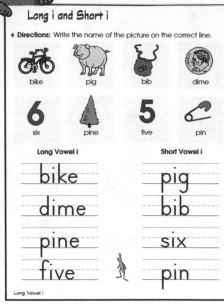

bike　pig　bib　dime

six　pine　five　pin

Long Vowel i	Short Vowel i
bike	pig
dime	bib
pine	six
five	pin

Long Vowel i

66

Meet Long u

Listen for the sound of long **u** in **mule**. The letters **u__e** and **ue** usually stand for the long **u** sound.

♦ **Directions:** Circle the pictures whose names have the long **u** sound.

mule

Long Vowel u

67

Search and Color

♦ **Directions:** Each word in the box has the sound of long **u**. Color the picture that matches each word in the box.

mule　glue　cubes　flute

Long Vowel u

68

Meet Long o

Listen for the sound of long **o** in **rose**.

♦ **Directions:** Say the name of each picture. Decide whether the vowel sound you hear is long **o** or short **o**. Fill in the circle beside long **o** or short **o**.

rose

- ● Long o ○ Short o
- ○ Long o ● Short o
- ○ Long o ● Short o
- ● Long o ○ Short o
- ○ Long o ● Short o
- ● Long o ○ Short o
- ○ Long o ● Short o
- ● Long o ○ Short o
- ○ Long o ● Short o
- ● Long o ○ Short o
- ● Long o ○ Short o
- ○ Long o ● Short o

Long Vowel o

69

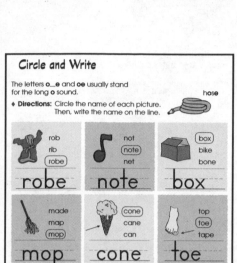

Circle and Write

The letters **o_e** and **oe** usually stand for the long **o** sound.

♦ **Directions:** Circle the name of each picture. Then, write the name on the line.

hose

rob / rib / (robe)	not / (note) / net	(box) / bike / bone
robe	**note**	**box**
made / map / (mop)	(cone) / cane / can	top / (toe) / tape
mop	**cone**	**toe**
bite / (bone) / bin	date / dig / (dog)	(rope) / ripe / rip
bone	**dog**	**rope**

Long Vowel o

70

Meet Long e

Listen for the sound of long **e** in **bee**. The letters **ee** and **ea** usually stand for the long **e** sound.

♦ **Directions:** Write the name of the picture on the correct line.

bee

seal | 10 | beet | jeep | leaf
bed | red | seat | feet

ee	ea	Short Vowel e
beet	seal	ten
jeep	leaf	bed
feet	seat	red

Long Vowel e

71

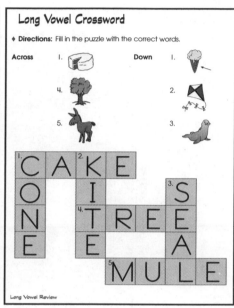

Long Vowel Crossword

♦ **Directions:** Fill in the puzzle with the correct words.

Across
1.
4.
5.

Down
1.
2.
3.

```
C A K E
O     I     S
N   T R E E
E     E   A
    M U L E
```

Long Vowel Review

72

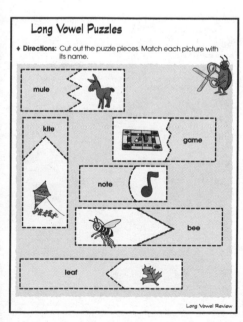

Long Vowel Puzzles

♦ **Directions:** Cut out the puzzle pieces. Match each picture with its name.

mule
kite
game
note
kite
bee
leaf

Long Vowel Review

73

Good Job!

The Sounds of y

A **y** at the end of a word can have the long **i** sound or the long **e** sound. Listen for the long **i** sound in **fly**. Listen for the long **e** sound in **pony**.

fly   pony

♦ **Directions:** Say the name of each picture. Listen for the sound of **y** at the end of the word. Circle either long **i** or long **e**.

sky — (Long i) Long e	baby — Long i (Long e)	bunny — Long i (Long e)
cry — (Long i) Long e	penny — Long i (Long e)	muddy — Long i (Long e)
dry — (Long i) Long e	twenty — Long i (Long e)	city — Long i (Long e)

y as a Vowel

75

317

Answer Key

Which Sound of y?

♦ **Directions:** Say the name of each picture. If the final **y** stands for the long **e** sound, color the picture green. If the **y** stands for the long **i** sound, color the picture yellow.

pony | fly | fifty
candy | dry | penny
cherry | sky | bunny

y as a Vowel

76

Sounds of c and g

Consonants **c** and **g** each have two sounds. Listen for the soft **c** sound in **pencil**. Listen for the hard **c** sound in **cup**.

Listen for the soft **g** sound in **giant**. Listen for the hard **g** sound in **goat**. **C** and **g** usually have the soft sound when they are followed by **e, i** or **y**.

♦ **Directions:** Say the name of each picture. Listen for the sound of **c** or **g**. Then, read the words in each list. Circle the words that have that sound of **c** or **g**.

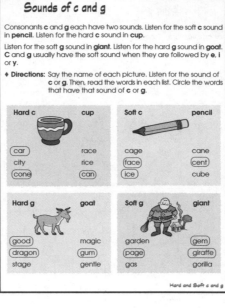

Hard c — cup
car | race
city | rice
cone | can

Soft c — pencil
cage | cane
face | cent
ice | cube

Hard g — goat
good | magic
dragon | gum
stage | gentle

Soft g — giant
garden | gem
page | giraffe
gas | gorilla

Hard and Soft c and g

77

Hard and Soft c and g

♦ **Directions:** Underline the letter that follows the **c** or **g** in each word. Write **hard** if the word has the hard **c** or hard **g** sound. Write **soft** if the word has the soft **c** or soft **g** sound.

car — hard | wagon — hard | cup — hard
pencil — soft | gym — soft | cot — hard
giant — soft | gem — soft | celery — soft
gum — soft | cymbals — soft | goat — soft
hard | soft | hard

Hard and Soft c and g

78

Consonant Blends With r

Sometimes two consonants at the beginning of a word blend together. Listen for the **dr** blend in **dragon**. **Gr, fr, cr, tr, br** and **pr** are also **r** blends.

dragon

♦ **Directions:** Draw a line from each consonant blend to the picture whose name begins with the same sound.

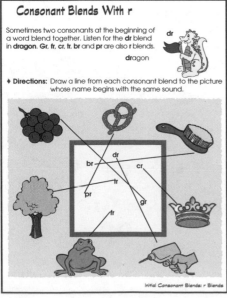

dr
br
cr
tr
pr
gr
fr

Initial Consonant Blends: r Blends

79

Fill the Tray

♦ **Directions:** Read the menu. Circle the words that have **r** blends. On the tray, draw pictures of the foods whose names you circled.

bread | pretzel | meat
butter | milk | grapes
salad | French fries | ice cream

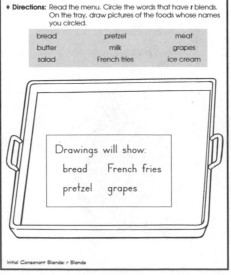

Drawings will show:
bread   French fries
pretzel grapes

Initial Consonant Blends: r Blends

80

Consonant Blends With l

Listen for the **cl** blend in **clown**. **Gl, pl, fl** and **bl** are also **l** blends.

clown

♦ **Directions:** Look at the **l** blend at the beginning of each row. Color the picture whose name begins with that sound.

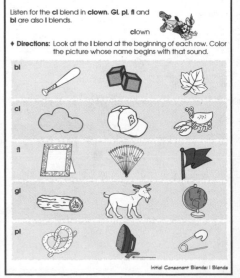

bl
cl
fl
gl
pl

Initial Consonant Blends: l Blends

81

Answer Key

318

L Blend Tic-Tac-Toe

♦ **Directions:** Color the pictures whose names begin with **l** blends. Draw a line through three colored pictures in a row to score a Tic-Tac-Toe.

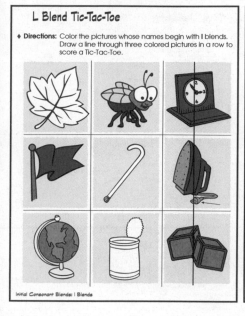

Initial Consonant Blends: l Blends

82

Consonant Blends With s

Listen for the **sk** blend in **skunk**. **Sm, st, sp, sw, sc, squ, sl** and **sn** are also **s** blends.

skunk

♦ **Directions:** Say the name of each picture. Circle the **s** blend you hear at the beginning of the name.

Initial Consonant Blends: s Blends

83

Match Pictures and Blends

♦ **Directions:** Draw a line from each **s** blend to the picture whose name begins with that sound.

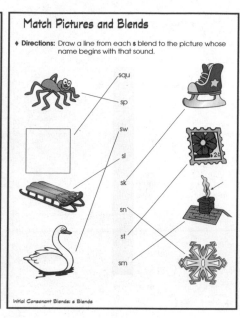

Initial Consonant Blends: s Blends

84

Blends at the Ends

Some consonant blends come at the ends of words. Listen for the **nd** blend at the end of the word **round**. **Mp, ng, nt, sk, nk** and **st** can also be ending blends.

round

♦ **Directions:** Say the name of each picture. Circle the blend you hear at the end of the name.

Final Blends

85

Follow the Final Blends

♦ **Directions:** Find the notes with pictures whose names end with consonant blends. Color them yellow. Draw a line through the yellow notes from the band to the tent.

Final Blends

86

Missing Blends

♦ **Directions:** Fill in the circle beside the missing blend in each word.

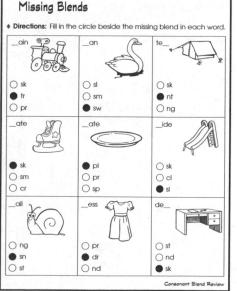

Consonant Blend Review

87

Answer Key

More Missing Blends

♦ **Directions:** Fill in the circle beside the missing blend in each word.

ri___	___y	___apes
○ nt	○ sl	● gr
○ st	● fl	○ cl
● ng	○ pl	○ sk
___obe	ha___	___og
○ sl	● nd	○ gr
● gl	○ ng	○ tr
○ gr	○ sk	● fr
___y	___ider	la___
● sk	○ pr	○ st
○ sm	○ sl	● mp
○ nt	● sp	○ ng

Consonant Blend Review

88

Consonant Digraph th

Some consonants work together to stand for a new sound. They are called **consonant digraphs**. Listen for the sound of consonant digraph **th** in **think**.

think

♦ **Directions:** Print **th** under the pictures whose names begin with the sound of **th**. Color the **th** pictures.

Initial Digraph th

89

Think About th

♦ **Directions:** Say the name of each picture. Fill in the missing letter or letters.

think	horn	thorn
10 ten	thumb	**30** thirty

♦ **Directions:** Find and circle these **th** words in the puzzle. The words may go **across** or **down**.

| think | thorn | thumb | thirty |

Initial Digraph th

90

Consonant Digraph sh

Listen for the sound of consonant digraph **sh** in **sheep**.

♦ **Directions:** Color the pictures whose names begin with the sound of **sh**.

sheep

Initial Digraph sh

91

Change a Word

♦ **Directions:** Make a new word by changing the beginning sound to **sh**. Write the new word on the line.

made - m + sh = shade

zip	sell	beep
ship	shell	sheep
tin	line	lift
shin	shine	shift
red	cape	cave
shed	shape	shave
top	bake	feet
shop	shake	sheet

Initial Digraph sh

92

Consonant Digraph wh

♦ **Directions:** Write **wh**, **th** or **sh** to complete each word.

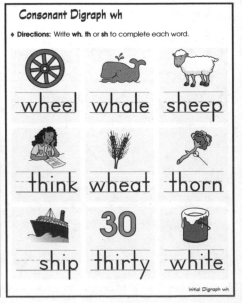

wheel · whale · sheep
think · wheat · thorn
ship · thirty · white

Initial Digraph wh

93

Answer Key

320

Wheel of Fortune

Listen for the sound of consonant digraph **wh** in **whale**.

whale

♦ **Directions:** Color the pictures whose names begin with consonant digraph **wh**.

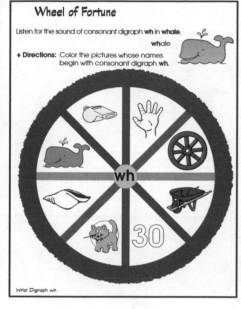

Initial Digraph wh

94

Consonant Digraph ch

Listen for the sound of consonant digraph **ch** in **cherry**.

cherry

♦ **Directions:** Trace the cherry if the name of the picture begins with the **ch** sound. Use a red crayon.

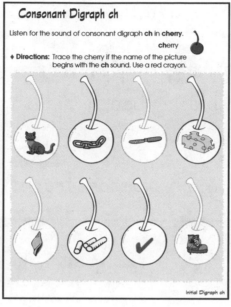

Initial Digraph ch

95

Read and Write ch

♦ **Directions:** Write a word from the box to label each picture.

chest	check	sheep
chimp	cherry	thirty
chain	cheese	wheel

cherry sheep chain
chest wheel cheese
chimp thirty check

Initial Digraph ch

96

Consonant Digraph kn

Listen for the sound of consonant digraph **kn** in **knot**. The **k** is silent.

knot

♦ **Directions:** Color the pictures whose names begin with the **kn** sound. Connect all the colored pictures from the knight to his horse.

Initial Digraph kn

97

Consonant Digraph wr

Listen for the sound of consonant digraph **wr** in **wren**. The **w** is silent.

wren

♦ **Directions:** Write a word from the box to label each picture. Color the pictures whose names begin with **wr**.

| web | wrist | wring | wrap |
| worm | write | wreath | wink | wrench |

wreath wrap worm
wrist wrench web
wink write wring

Initial Digraph wr

98

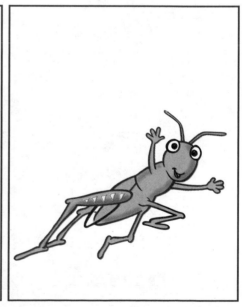

Answer Key

Ending Digraphs

Some words end with consonant digraphs. Listen for the ending digraphs in **duck**, **moth**, **dish** and **branch**.

duck   moth   dish   branch

♦ **Directions:** Say the name of each picture. Circle the letters that stand for the ending sound.

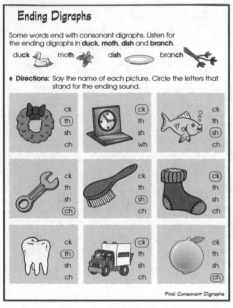

ck / **(th)** / sh / ch	**(ck)** / th / sh / wh	ck / th / **(sh)** / ch
ck / th / sh / **(ch)**	ck / th / **(sh)** / ch	**(ck)** / th / sh / ch
ck / **(th)** / sh / ch	**(ck)** / th / sh / ch	ck / th / sh / **(ch)**

Final Consonant Digraphs

99

Hear and Write Digraphs

♦ **Directions:** Write **ck**, **th**, **sh** or **ch** to complete each word.

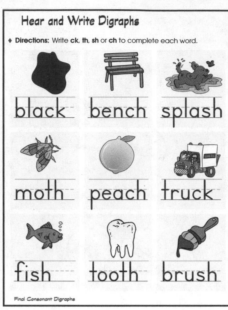

black	bench	splash
moth	peach	truck
fish	tooth	brush

Final Consonant Digraphs

100

Missing Digraphs

♦ **Directions:** Fill in the circle beside the missing digraph in each word.

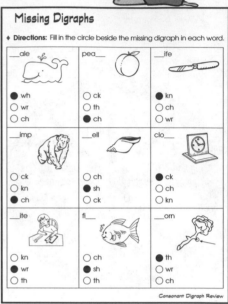

__ale	pea__	__ife
● wh / ○ wr / ○ ch	○ ck / ○ th / ● ch	● kn / ○ ch / ○ wr
__imp	__ell	clo__
○ ck / ○ kn / ● ch	○ ch / ● sh / ○ ck	● ck / ○ ch / ○ kn
__ite	fi__	__orn
○ kn / ● wr / ○ th	○ ch / ● sh / ○ th	● th / ○ wr / ○ ch

Consonant Digraph Review

101

Missing Digraphs

♦ **Directions:** Fill in the circle beside the missing digraph in each word.

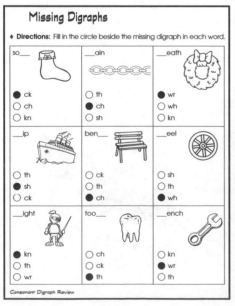

so__	__ain	__eath
● ck / ○ ch / ○ kn	○ th / ● ch / ○ sh	● wr / ○ wh / ○ kn
__ip	ben__	__eel
○ th / ● sh / ○ ck	○ ck / ○ th / ● ch	○ sh / ○ th / ● wh
__ight	too__	__ench
● kn / ○ th / ○ wr	○ ch / ○ ck / ● th	○ kn / ● wr / ○ th

Consonant Digraph Review

102

Tricky ar

When **r** follows a vowel, it changes the vowel's sound. Listen for the **ar** sound in **star**.

star

♦ **Directions:** Color the pictures whose names have the **ar** sound.

r-Controlled Vowels

103

Write ar or or

Listen for the **or** sound in **horn**.

horn

♦ **Directions:** Write **ar** or **or** to complete each word.

thorn	cart	forty
stork	corn	harp
arm	star	porch

r-Controlled Vowels

104

Answer Key

322

Mix and Match

The letters **ur**, **er** and **ir** all have the same sound. Listen for the vowel sound in **surf**, **fern** and **girl**.

surf   fern   girl

♦ **Directions:** Draw a line from each word in the circle to the picture it names.

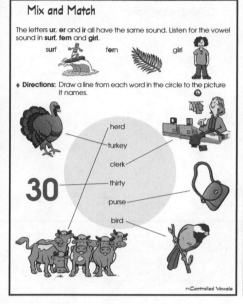

30

herd
turkey
clerk
thirty
purse
bird

r-Controlled Vowels

105

Write ur, er and ir

♦ **Directions:** Find a word from the box to name each picture. Write it on the line below the picture.

| church | clerk | dirt | fern |
| girl | herd | purple | surf | thirty |

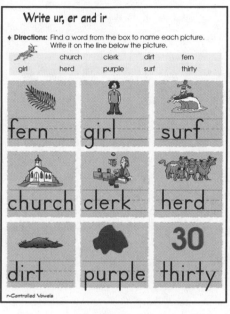

fern   girl   surf

church   clerk   herd

dirt   purple   thirty

r-Controlled Vowels

106

Rhyme Time

♦ **Directions:** Cut out the words at the bottom of the page. Glue them beside the words they rhyme with.

barn | yarn   corn | horn

purse | nurse   skirt | shirt

bird | herd   girl | curl

star | car   cork | fork

r-Controlled Vowels

107

Vowel Pairs ai and ay

You know that the letters **a_e** usually stand for the long **a** sound. The vowel pairs **ai** and **ay** can stand for the long **a** sound, too. Listen for the long **a** sound in **train** and **hay**.

♦ **Directions:** Say the name of each picture below. Look at the vowel pair that stands for the long **a** sound. Under each picture, write the words from the box that have the same long **a** vowel pair.

cage	chain	gate	gray
mail	pay	snail	skate
play	snake	stay	tail

cake   train   hay

cage   chain   gray
gate   mail   pay
skate   snail   play
snake   tail   stay

Vowel Pairs

109

Vowel Pairs oa and ow

You know that the letters **o_e** and **oe** usually stand for the long **o** sound. The vowel pairs **oa** and **ow** can stand for the long **o** sound, too. Listen for the long **o** sound in **road** and **snow**.

♦ **Directions:** Find and circle eight long **o** words. The words may go **across** or **down**. Beside each picture, write the words that use the same long **o** vowel pair.

Z	L	I	A	C	R
O	W	R	J	A	W
S	G	O	A	L	G
O	A	L	A	G	R
A	L	A	G	X	O
P	Y	K	N	O	W

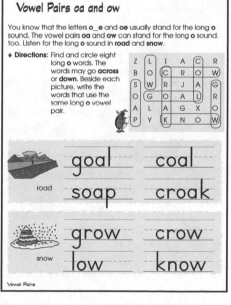

road   goal   coal
         soap   croak

snow   grow   crow
         low   know

Vowel Pairs

110

Vowel Pair ui

You know that the letters **u_e** and **ue** usually stand for the long **u** sound. The vowel pair **ui** can stand for the long **u** sound, too. Listen for the long **u** sound in **cruise**.

♦ **Directions:** Circle the name of the picture. Then, write the name on the line.

cruise

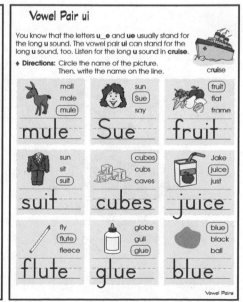

mall, male, **mule**	sun, **Sue**, say	**fruit**, flat, frame
mule	Sue	fruit
sun, sit, **suit**	**cubes**, cubs, caves	Jake, **juice**, just
suit	cubes	juice
fly, **flute**, fleece	globe, gull, **glue**	**blue**, black, ball
flute	glue	blue

Vowel Pairs

111

Answer Key

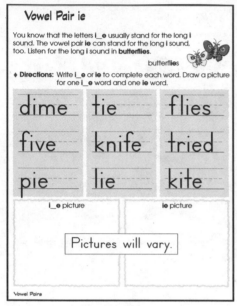

Vowel Pair ie

You know that the letters i_e usually stand for the long i sound. The vowel pair ie can stand for the long i sound, too. Listen for the long i sound in **butterflies**.

butterflies

♦ **Directions:** Write i_e or ie to complete each word. Draw a picture for one i_e word and one ie word.

dime	tie	flies
five	knife	tried
pie	lie	kite

i_e picture	ie picture
Pictures will vary.	

Vowel Pairs

112

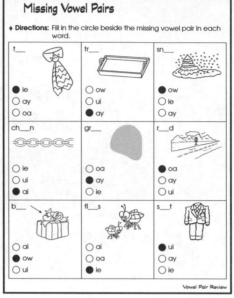

Missing Vowel Pairs

♦ **Directions:** Fill in the circle beside the missing vowel pair in each word.

t__ ● ie ○ ay ○ oa
tr__ ○ ow ○ ui ● ay
sn__ ● ow ○ ie ○ ay
ch__n ○ ie ○ ui ● ai
gr__ ○ oa ● ay ○ ie
r__d ● oa ○ ay ○ ui
b__ ○ ai ● ow ○ ui
fl__s ○ ai ○ oa ● ie
s__t ● ui ○ ai ○ ie

Vowel Pair Review

113

Missing Vowel Pairs

♦ **Directions:** Fill in the circle beside the missing vowel pair in each word.

h__ ○ ui ○ ow ● ay
tr__n ○ oa ● ai ○ ie
s__p ● oa ○ ai ○ ui
j__ce ○ ai ● ui ○ ie
p__ ○ ui ○ oa ● ie
cr__ ○ ui ○ ay ● ow
g__t ○ ai ● oa ○ ui
fr__t ● ai ○ ow ○ ui
sn__l ○ ow ● ai ○ ie

Vowel Pair Review

114

Vowel Pair ea

Some pairs of vowels can stand for more than one sound. The vowel pair **ea** has the sound of long e in **team** and short e in **head**.

team   head

♦ **Directions:** Say the name of each picture. Listen for the sound that **ea** stands for. Circle **Long e** or **Short e**. Then, color the pictures whose names have the short e sound.

Long e · Short e   Long e · (Short e)   (Long e) · Short e
(Long e) · Short e   Long e · (Short e)   (Long e) · Short e
Long e · (Short e)   (Long e) · Short e   Long e · (Short e)

Vowel Pairs

115

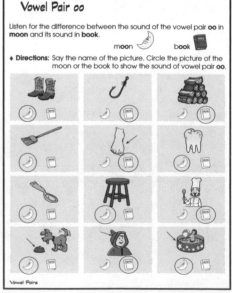

Vowel Pair oo

Listen for the difference between the sound of the vowel pair **oo** in **moon** and its sound in **book**.

moon   book

♦ **Directions:** Say the name of the picture. Circle the picture of the moon or the book to show the sound of vowel pair oo.

Vowel Pairs

116

Answer Key

324

Make Compound Words

Some short words can be put together to make one new word. The new word is called a **compound word**.

cow + hand = cowhand

♦ **Directions:** Look at each pair of pictures and words below. Join the two words to make a compound word. Write it on the line.

rain + coat = **raincoat**

door + bell = **doorbell**

dog + house = **doghouse**

pan + cake = **pancake**

horse + shoe = **horseshoe**

Compound Words

117

Compound Word Riddles

♦ **Directions:** Underline the two words in each sentence that can make a compound word. Write the compound word on the line to complete the sentence.

A kind of bird that is black is a
blackbird

A horse that can race is a
racehorse

A cloth that covers a table is a
tablecloth

A room with a bed is a
bedroom

A book with a story is a
storybook

A bowl that holds fish is a
fishbowl

Compound Words

118

Build Words With Syllables

Syllables are word parts. Each syllable has one vowel sound. Some words have only one syllable. Some words have more than one syllable.

One syllable: kite   **Two syllables:** wagon

♦ **Directions:** Cut out the syllables at the bottom of the page. Put them together to make eight two-syllable words. Look up the words in a dictionary to check their spellings. Then, write the words you made.

My 2-Syllable Word Record

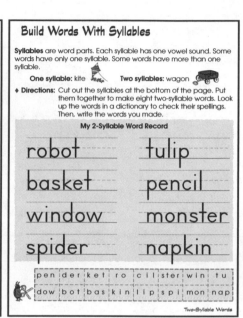

robot   tulip

basket   pencil

window   monster

spider   napkin

pen	der	ket	ro	cil	ster	win	tu
dow	bot	bas	kin	lip	spi	mon	nap

Two-Syllable Words

119

Prefix re

A **prefix** is a word part. It is added to the beginning of a base word to change the base word's meaning. The prefix **re** means "again."

Example: **Refill** means "to fill again."

♦ **Directions:** Look at the pictures. Read the base words. Add the prefix **re** to the base word to show that the action is being done again. Write your new word on the line.

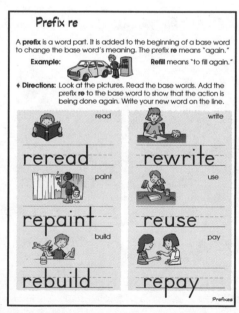

read   **reread**

write   **rewrite**

paint   **repaint**

use   **reuse**

build   **rebuild**

pay   **repay**

Prefixes

121

Prefixes un and dis

The prefixes **un** and **dis** mean "not" or "the opposite of."
Unlocked means "not locked."   **Dismount** is the "opposite of mount."

♦ **Directions:** Look at the pictures. Circle the word that tells about the picture. Then, write the word on the line.

tied   (untied)

like   (dislike)

untied   **dislike**

happy   (unhappy)

obey   (disobey)

happy   **obey**

safe   (unsafe)

honest   (dishonest)

unsafe   **dishonest**

Prefixes

122

Suffixes ful, less, ness, ly

A **suffix** is a word part that is added at the end of a base word to change the base word's meaning. Look at the suffixes below.

The suffix **ful** means "full of." **Cheerful** means "full of cheer."

The suffix **less** means "without." **Cloudless** means "without clouds."

The suffix **ness** means "a state of being." **Darkness** means "being dark."

The suffix **ly** means "in this way." **Slowly** means "in a slow way."

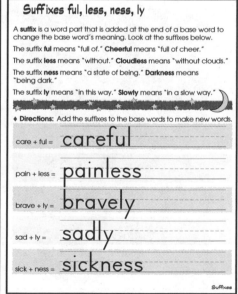

♦ **Directions:** Add the suffixes to the base words to make new words.

care + ful = **careful**

pain + less = **painless**

brave + ly = **bravely**

sad + ly = **sadly**

sick + ness = **sickness**

Suffixes

123

Answer Key

Suffixes and Meanings

Remember: The suffix **ful** means "full of."
The suffix **less** means "without."
The suffix **ness** means "a state of being."
The suffix **ly** means "in this way."

The sun shines **brightly**.

♦ **Directions:** Write the word that matches the meaning.

without pain	in a neat way
painless	neatly

full of grace	the state of being sick
graceful	sickness

in a quick way	without fear
quickly	fearless

the state of being soft	in a glad way
softness	gladly

Suffixes

124

Suffixes er and est

Suffixes **er** and **est** can be used to compare. Use **er** when you compare two things. Use **est** when you compare more than two things.

Example: The puppy is smaller than its mom. This puppy is the small**est** puppy in the litter.

♦ **Directions:** Add the suffixes to the base words to make words that compare.

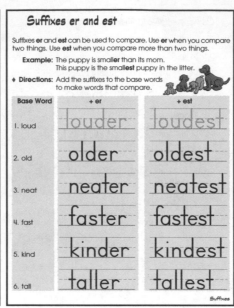

Base Word	+ er	+ est
1. loud	louder	loudest
2. old	older	oldest
3. neat	neater	neatest
4. fast	faster	fastest
5. kind	kinder	kindest
6. tall	taller	tallest

Suffixes

125

Compare With er and est

♦ **Directions:** Use **er** and **est** to compare things in three pictures.

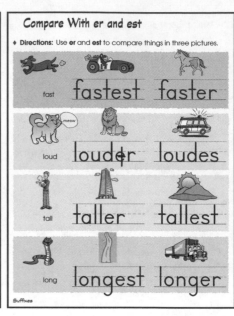

fast	fastest	faster
loud	louder	loudes
tall	taller	tallest
long	longest	longer

Suffixes

126

READING COMPREHENSION

Three Little Bugs

Use the Clues

Context clues can help you figure out words you don't know. Read the words around the new word. Think of a word that makes sense.

Kate swam in a _____?

Did Kate swim in a cake or a lake? The word **swim** is a context clue.

♦ **Directions:** Kate wrote this letter from camp. Read the letter. Use context clues to write the missing words from the word box. What clues did you use?

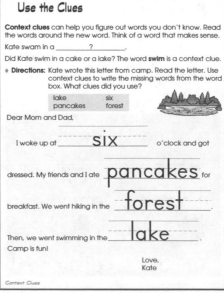

lake	six
pancakes	forest

Dear Mom and Dad,

I woke up at __six__ o'clock and got

dressed. My friends and I ate __pancakes__ for

breakfast. We went hiking in the __forest__.

Then, we went swimming in the __lake__.
Camp is fun!

Love,
Kate

Context Clues

130

Clues for Clothes

♦ **Directions:** _____ words. Write the words from the word box. Then, answer the questions.

socks	scarf	sweaters	mittens

Maria bundles up. She sticks her arms through

two __sweaters__. She tugs three pairs of

__socks__ over her feet. She wraps a __scarf__
Read the story. Use context clues to figure out the missing

around her neck. At last, she pulls her __mittens__
onto her hands. Maria goes outside to play. Nobody is warmer
than Maria.

1. What clue words helped you figure out sweaters?

__sticks her arms through__

2. What clue words helped you figure out mittens?

__onto her hands__

Context Clues

131

Context Clues in Action

♦ **Directions:** Read the story. Use context clues to figure out the meanings of the words in dark print. Draw a line from the word to its meaning.

Jack has a plan. He wants to take his parents out to lunch to show that he **appreciates** all the nice things they do for him. His sister Jessica will go, too, so she won't feel left out. Jack is **thrifty**. He saves the **allowance** he earns for doing **chores** around the house. So far, Jack has saved ten dollars. He needs only five dollars more. He is excited about paying the check himself. He will feel like an **adult**.

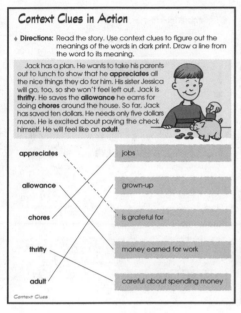

appreciates	jobs
allowance	grown-up
chores	is grateful for
thrifty	money earned for work
adult	careful about spending money

Context Clues

132

Amazing Antonyms

Antonyms are words that have opposite meanings. **Old** and **new** are antonyms. **Laugh** and **cry** are antonyms, too.

♦ **Directions:** Below each word, write its antonym. Use words from the word box.

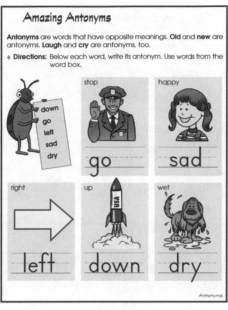

down
go
left
sad
dry

stop — go
happy — sad
right — left
up — down
wet — dry

Antonyms

133

Scale the Synonym Slope

Synonyms are words that have almost the same meaning. **Tired** and **sleepy** are synonyms. **Talk** and **speak** are synonyms.

♦ **Directions:** Read the word. Find its synonym on the hill. Write the synonym on the line.

1. glad — happy
2. little — small
3. begin — start
4. above — over
5. damp — wet
6. large — big

Synonyms

134

Synonym Match

♦ **Directions:** Look at the pictures. Read the words in the box. Write two synonyms you could use to tell about each picture.

rocks start road begin street stones sad unhappy

sad
unhappy

rocks
stones

road
street

start
begin

Synonyms

135

Antonym or Synonym?

♦ **Directions:** Use yellow to color the spaces that have word pairs that are antonyms. Use blue to color the spaces that have word pairs that are synonyms.

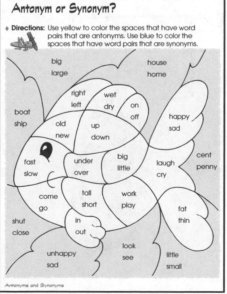

Antonyms and Synonyms

136

Homophone Fun

Homophones are words that sound the same but have different spellings and meanings. **Too** and **two** are homophones. So are **road** and **rode**.

♦ **Directions:** Use yellow to color the balloons that have homophones.

Homophones

137

Answer Key

Find the Right Homophone

♦ **Directions:** Read the sentences. Write the correct homophone on the line.

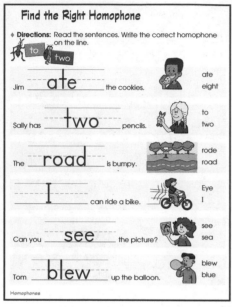

Jim __ate__ the cookies. ate eight

Sally has __two__ pencils. to two

The __road__ is bumpy. rode road

__I__ can ride a bike. Eye I

Can you __see__ the picture? see sea

Tom __blew__ up the balloon. blew blue

Homophones

138

Color Code Classifying

♦ **Directions:** Underline **number words** in red.
Underline **name words** in blue.
Underline **color words** in green.
Underline **animal words** in yellow.

pig	Kim	dog	blue
red	green	ten	five
Jack	two	cow	Lee

♦ **Directions:** Write each word on the correct line.

Name Words

Kim   Jack   Lee

Number Words

two   ten   five

Animal Words

dog   pig   cow

Color Words

green   blue   red

Classifying

139

Menu Mix-Up

♦ **Directions:** Circle **names of vegetables** in green.
Circle **names of drinks** in red.
Circle **names of desserts** in pink.

♦ **Directions:** Write each food word on the correct line.

Drinks	Vegetables	Desserts
milk	corn	pie
water	carrot	cookie
juice	peas	cake

Classifying

140

Sort It Out

♦ **Directions:** Color the pictures. Cut and glue each picture in the correct room.

141

Good Job!

Word Sort

♦ **Directions:** Circle words that name **colors** in red.
Circle words that name **shapes** in yellow.
Circle words that name **numbers** in green.

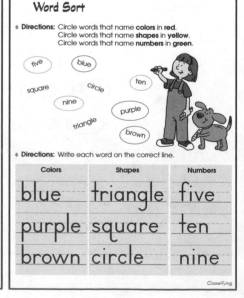

five   blue
square   circle   ten
nine   purple
triangle   brown

♦ **Directions:** Write each word on the correct line.

Colors	Shapes	Numbers
blue	triangle	five
purple	square	ten
brown	circle	nine

Classifying

143

Answer Key

328

Where Does It Belong?

◆ **Directions:** Read the words.
Draw a **circle** around the **sky words**.
Draw a **line** under the **land words**.
Draw a **box** around the **sea words**.

Sky Words: cloud moon planet

Land Words: forest city rabbit

Sea Words: whale shark shell

Classifying

144

What's the Big Idea?

The **main idea** is the most important idea in a story. The main idea tells what happens.

◆ **Directions:** Look at the pictures. Read the sentences. Circle **yes** if the sentence tells the main idea of the picture. Circle **no** if it does not.

Main Idea

145

Find the Main Idea

◆ **Directions:** Look at the pictures. Read the sentences. In the circle, write the letter of the sentence that tells the main idea.

A. The eggs are ready to hatch.
B. It is a very windy day.
C. The old house looks scary.
D. The popcorn popper is too full.
E. The girl thinks the music is too loud.
F. It is too warm for a snowman.

Main Idea

146

What's the Idea?

◆ **Directions:** Look at the pictures. Read the sentences in the speech balloons. Fill in the circle beside the sentence that tells the main idea.

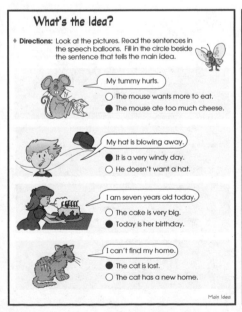

Main Idea

147

Read All About It

◆ **Directions:** Read each part of the paper. Fill in the circle beside the sentence that tells the main idea.

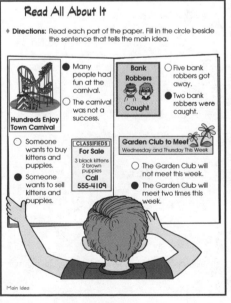

Main Idea

148

What Doesn't Belong?

◆ **Directions:** Read the sentences under each title. Cross out the sentence that does not tell about the main idea.

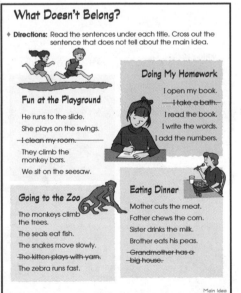

Main Idea

149

Answer Key

Main Ideas About Meals

♦ **Directions:** Read each story to find the main idea. Fill in the circle beside the phrase that tells the main idea.

Open Wide!

An anteater slowly walked up to a log. Many ants were inside the log. The anteater put on a bib. Then, she laid a plate and a big spoon down on the ground. She began to eat and eat. When she was finished, she had eaten 30,000 ants!

○ many ants
○ a log on the ground
● a hungry anteater

Bite Down!

It's a good thing that Rollo Rabbit likes to chew. He nibbles on carrots, lettuce, and cabbage all day long. Every time he chews, he wears down his teeth. If Rollo did not chew so much, his front teeth could grow to be ten feet long!

○ good vegetables
● wearing down teeth
○ a fluffy rabbit

Main Idea

150

Storyboard Sequence

Sequence is the order in which story events happen. What happened first? What happened next? What happened last?

♦ **Directions:** Write the numbers 1, 2 and 3 in the boxes to show the order in which the story events in each row happened.

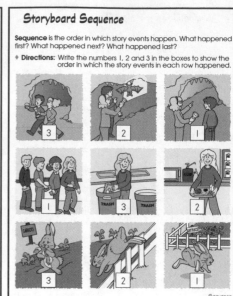

Sequence

151

Words in Order

♦ **Directions:** Look at each picture. Write 1, 2 and 3 to make the words tell a story in order.

1	mix	2	give
3	eat	3	open
2	bake	1	buy

2	fly	2	read
3	land	1	open
1	take off	3	close

2	listen	2	hurt
3	turn off	1	fall
1	turn on	3	bandage

Sequence

152

Story Sequence

♦ **Directions:** Read the story.

"Heads for Boston!" "Tails for Portland!"

Over a hundred years ago, two men built a town. They couldn't decide what to name it. One man wanted to name it Boston. The other wanted to name it Portland. They tossed a coin and one yelled, "Heads for Boston!" The other yelled, "Tails for Portland!" Tails must have won because that town is now called Portland, Oregon.

♦ **Directions:** Read the sentences. Write 1, 2, 3 and 4 to number the events in the order they happened in the story.

built a town.

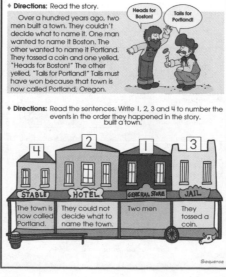

4 STABLE	2 HOTEL	1 GENERAL STORE	3 JAIL
The town is now called Portland.	They could not decide what to name the town.	Two men	They tossed a coin.

Sequence

153

Otter Order

♦ **Directions:** Read the story.

A sea otter eats clams, barnacles, worms, sea urchins and abalone. First, it must dive underwater to find its food. After bringing the food to the surface, the sea otter rolls onto its back and puts the food on its belly. It keeps its "picnic table" clean by rolling in the water to wash away any messy scraps. Sea otters are very neat eaters!

♦ **Directions:** Write the number 1, 2, 3, 4 or 5 in each box to tell the order in which the sea otter eats a meal.

It rolls in the water

4 The sea otter puts its food on its belly.	2 The sea otter brings its food to the surface.	3 It rolls onto its back.
5 to wash away messy scraps.		1 The sea otter dives underwater to find its food.

Sequencing

154

Lemonade for Sale

♦ **Directions:** Read the story.

Ken and Pat start a business selling lemonade. First, they make a stand from Pat's picnic table. Second, they go to the store to buy a box of lemons and a sack of sugar. Third, they squeeze the lemons and pick out the seeds. Fourth, they mix the lemon juice with sugar and cold water. Would you like to buy a cold glass of lemonade from them? It's only fifteen cents.

♦ **Directions:** Read the phrases. Write 1, 2, 3 and 4 to number the phrases in the order they happened in the story. Clue words like **first** will help you.

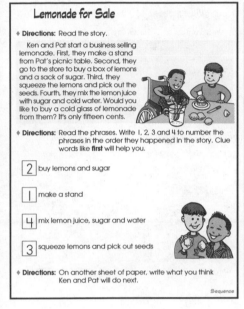

2 buy lemons and sugar

1 make a stand

4 mix lemon juice, sugar and water

3 squeeze lemons and pick out seeds

♦ **Directions:** On another sheet of paper, write what you think Ken and Pat will do next.

Sequence

155

A Hare-Raising Experience

♦ **Directions:** Read the story.

Jack Rabbit loved to grow carrots. First, he found a diamond-shaped field. Next, he carefully planted and watered the seeds. Then he watched as the little green tops of carrots began pushing through the dirt. Finally, 83 carrots were ready to be pulled from the earth. Jack indeed had the only 83-"carrot" diamond in town, and he proudly gave it to his friend Jill.

♦ **Directions:** Read the sentences. Write 1, 2, 3, 4 or 5 to number the sentences in the order they happened in the story.

5 The carrots were ready to be pulled.

4 Carrot tops started popping up.

1 Jack found a field.

3 Jack watered the seeds.

2 Jack planted carrot seeds.

♦ **Directions:** On another sheet of paper, write what you think will happen next.

Sequence

156

Fun With Directions

♦ **Directions:** Follow the number code to color the balloons. Color the clown, too.

| 1 — blue | 2 — orange | 3 — yellow | 4 — green | 5 — purple |
| 6 — brown | 7 — red | 8 — black | 9 — blue | 10 — purple |

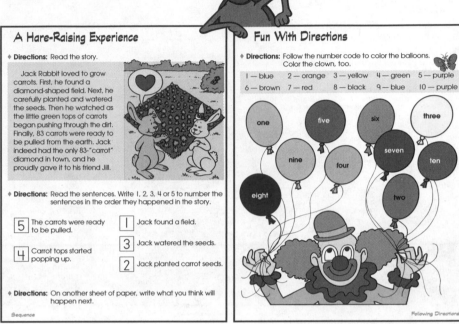

one, five, six, three, nine, four, seven, ten, eight, two

Following Directions

157

Draw With Directions

♦ **Directions:** Follow the directions to complete the picture.

1. Draw a smiling yellow face on the sun.
2. Color the fish blue. Draw 2 more blue fish in the water.
3. Draw a brown bird under the cloud. Draw blue raindrops under the cloud.
4. Color the boat purple. Color one sail orange. Color the other sail green.
5. Color the starfish yellow. Draw 2 more yellow starfish.

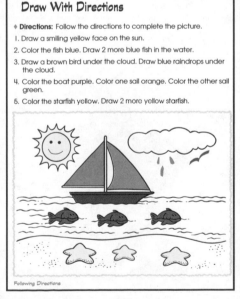

Following Directions

158

Directions for Decorating

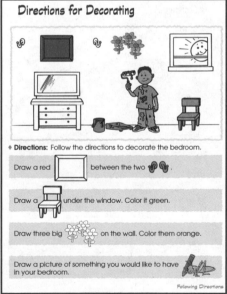

♦ **Directions:** Follow the directions to decorate the bedroom.

Draw a red ☐ between the two 🩴.

Draw a chair under the window. Color it green.

Draw three big 🌼 on the wall. Color them orange.

Draw a picture of something you would like to have in your bedroom.

Following Directions

159

Skateboard Course

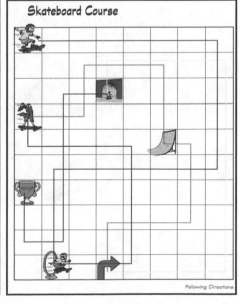

Following Directions

161

Answer Key

What Is It?

When you don't get the whole picture, you may need to **draw conclusions** for yourself. To draw a conclusion, think about what you see or read. Think about what you already know. Then, make a good guess.

♦ **Directions:** Look at each picture. Use what you know and what you see to draw a conclusion. Draw a line to the sentence that tells about each picture.

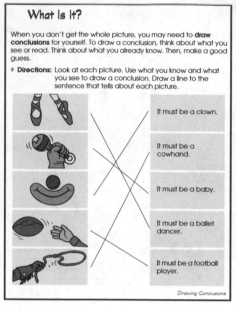

It must be a clown.

It must be a cowhand.

It must be a baby.

It must be a ballet dancer.

It must be a football player.

Drawing Conclusions

163

Who Said It?

♦ **Directions:** Use what you see, what you read and what you know to draw conclusions. Draw a line from the animal to what it might say.

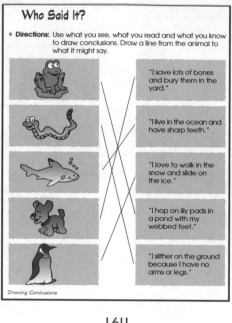

"I save lots of bones and bury them in the yard."

"I live in the ocean and have sharp teeth."

"I love to walk in the snow and slide on the ice."

"I hop on lily pads in a pond with my webbed feet."

"I slither on the ground because I have no arms or legs."

Drawing Conclusions

164

What Happened?

♦ **Directions:** Look at the pictures. Fill in the circle beside the sentence that tells what happened in the missing picture. Draw a picture that shows what happened.

What happened?

● The boy dropped the string.   ○ The boy took his kite home.

What happened?

○ The angry baby played in its bed.   ● The hungry baby drank the milk.

Drawing Conclusions

165

My Conclusion Is . . .

♦ **Directions:** Read the sentences. Look at the pictures. Circle the picture that completes the last sentence.

1. Emily is on a class trip. She sees cows eating grass and horses in the barn. Hens are sitting on their eggs. She must be visiting a . . .

2. Timmy wore his best suit. He sat in a tall chair. He combed his hair. A man said, "Say cheese!" The man is a . . .

3. Mark spilled milk on the floor. He had to clean up the mess. He went to the closet and got a . . .

Drawing Conclusions

166

I Conclude!

♦ **Directions:** Read each story. Fill in the circle beside the answer that completes the last sentence.

The little house is in the backyard. Inside is a bowl of water. Next to the bowl is a big bone. This house belongs to . . .

○ some birds.   ○ a family of elves.   ● a puppy.

The yellow cat is fluffy. The black cat is thin. The tan and white cat acts friendly. The little gray cat is shy. Cats are all . . .

● different.   ○ angry.   ○ silly.

Lois keeps her pet in an aquarium. Her pet can hop. It eats flies and is green. Her pet is . . .

○ a bunny.   ● a frog.   ○ very tall.

We played a game. We ran away from Sofia. When she tapped Raymond, he was it. We were playing . . .

○ soccer.   ○ basketball.   ● tag.

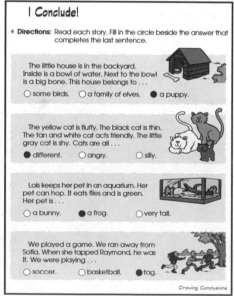

Drawing Conclusions

167

Answer Key

332

Clues to Conclusions

◆ **Directions:** Read each story. Fill in the circle beside the correct conclusion.

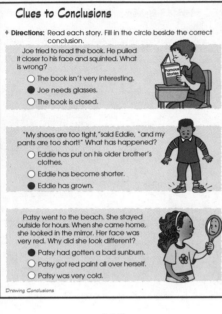

Joe tried to read the book. He pulled it closer to his face and squinted. What is wrong?

- ○ The book isn't very interesting.
- ● Joe needs glasses.
- ○ The book is closed.

"My shoes are too tight,"said Eddie, "and my pants are too short!" What has happened?

- ○ Eddie has put on his older brother's clothes.
- ○ Eddie has become shorter.
- ● Eddie has grown.

Patsy went to the beach. She stayed outside for hours. When she came home, she looked in the mirror. Her face was very red. Why did she look different?

- ● Patsy had gotten a bad sunburn.
- ○ Patsy got red paint all over herself.
- ○ Patsy was very cold.

Drawing Conclusions

168

Find the Facts

Facts and details tell more about the main idea. Facts and details give more information.

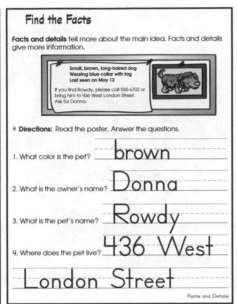

Small, brown, long-haired dog
Wearing blue collar with tag
Last seen on May 12

If you find Rowdy, please call 555-6702 or bring him to 436 West London Street. Ask for Donna.

◆ **Directions:** Read the poster. Answer the questions.

1. What color is the pet? **brown**

2. What is the owner's name? **Donna**

3. What is the pet's name? **Rowdy**

4. Where does the pet live? **436 West London Street**

Facts and Details

169

Facts About Fingerprints

◆ **Directions:** Read the story.

The lines and swirls on your fingertips make fingerprints. There are three fingerprint patterns. The first is called the loop. The second is the arch. The third is the whorl. Your fingerprints stay the same all your life. Each person's fingerprints are different.

loop
arch   whorl

◆ **Directions:** Read each sentence. Color the **True** ink pad if the sentence is true. Color the **False** ink pad if the sentence is false.

1. There are four fingerprint patterns. True / **False**

2. Your fingerprints change as you grow. True / **False**

3. Fingerprints are made from the lines and swirls on your fingertips. **True** / False

4. No one else has fingerprints exactly like yours. **True** / False

Facts and Details

170

Pictures in Detail

◆ **Directions:** Read the story.

The Aztecs in Mexico used straw to make pictures. First, they colored the straw using dyes made from plants. Next, they drew a design. Then, they cut the straw into small pieces. Finally, they glued each piece of straw to the design to form the picture.

◆ **Directions:** Complete the sentences with words from the story.

1. Aztecs in **Mexico** used straw to make **pictures**

2. Dyes were made from **plants**

3. The **straw** was cut into small pieces.

4. Each piece was **glued** to the **design**

Facts and Details

171

Details Wanted!

Here is a wanted poster about One-Eyed Harry who robbed a bank last night. Harry has a mean and beady eye. He wears a patch over his other eye just to scare people. He's about five feet tall and wears a polka-dot bandanna. He has a dirty beard and a long pointed nose with a wart on the tip. He wears an earring in one ear, and he has one gold front tooth.

Wanted

One-Eyed Harry

◆ **Directions:** Circle **Yes** or **No** to tell about the details.

Harry wears a polka-dot bandanna.	**Yes**	No
Harry has two kind eyes.	Yes	**No**
Harry has a long pointed nose.	**Yes**	No
Harry wears an earring in his nose.	Yes	**No**
Harry has a gold front tooth.	**Yes**	No

Facts and Details

172

Same and Different

Reading to find out how things are **alike** or **different** can help you picture and remember what you read. Things that are alike are called **similarities**. Things that are not alike are called **differences**.

Similarity: Beth and Michelle are both girls.
Difference: Beth has short hair, but Michelle has long hair.

◆ **Directions:** Read the story.

Michelle and Beth are wearing new dresses. Both dresses are striped and have four shiny buttons. Each dress has a belt and a pocket. Beth's dress is blue and white, while Michelle's is yellow and white. The stripes on Beth's dress go up and down. Stripes on Michelle's dress go from side to side. Beth's pocket is bigger with room for a kitten.

◆ **Directions:** Add the details. Color the dresses. Show how the dresses are alike and how they are different.

Beth's Dress   **Michelle's Dress**

Similarities and Differences

173

333

Answer Key

Comparing Cars

♦ **Directions:** Read the story.

Sarah built a car for a race. Sarah's car has wheels, a steering wheel and a place to sit just like the family car. It doesn't have a motor, a key or a gas pedal. Sarah came in second in last year's race. This year, she hopes to win the race.

♦ **Directions:** Write **S** beside the things Sarah's car has that are like things the family car has. Write **D** beside the things that are different.

S		steering wheel
D		motor
D		gas pedal
S		seat
S		wheels

Similarities and Differences

174

Making Inferences

Not every story tells you all the facts. Sometimes you need to put together details to understand what is happening in a story. When you put details together, you **make inferences.**

♦ **Directions:** Read each story. Fill in the circle beside the inference you can make from the details you have.

Everyone on the Pine School baseball team wears a blue shirt on Mondays. It is Monday and Brenda is wearing a blue shirt.
- ○ Brenda always wears blue clothes.
- ○ Brenda cannot find her red shirt.
- ● Brenda is on the baseball team.

My cat has brown and white stripes. It meows when it wants to be fed. My cat is meowing now.
- ○ The cat wants to go outside.
- ● The cat is hungry.
- ○ The cat doesn't like brown and white stripes.

Every afternoon the children run outside when they hear a bell ring. At 2:00, Mr. Chocovan drives by in his ice-cream truck. The children hear a bell ringing. They run outside.
- ● It is time for ice cream.
- ○ It is time for the children to go home.
- ○ It is time for a fire drill.

Making Inferences

177

Figure It Out

♦ **Directions:** Read the story.

It is a rainy day. Mom tells Tosh to stay inside until the weather clears up. Tosh lies on his bed and pouts. He sings one song over and over. Now and then, he checks to see if the rain has stopped.

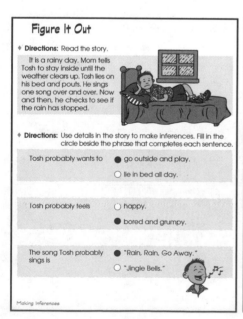

♦ **Directions:** Use details in the story to make inferences. Fill in the circle beside the phrase that completes each sentence.

Tosh probably wants to
- ● go outside and play.
- ○ lie in bed all day.

Tosh probably feels
- ○ happy.
- ● bored and grumpy.

The song Tosh probably sings is
- ● "Rain, Rain, Go Away."
- ○ "Jingle Bells."

Making Inferences

178

Inferences About Characters

♦ **Directions:** Read this story. Look for clues about Tom. Then, follow the directions below the story.

"You can't get me!" Goldie teased Tom when she saw him looking at her.
"I never said that I wanted to get you, anyway," answered Tom, knowing that Goldie was right. He walked away, waving his fluffy tail proudly.
Although Goldie had once been afraid of Tom, she now liked to tease him.
"It's fun to tease Tom. When he is upset, all his fur stands straight up," she thought.
Soon Goldie heard noises. Someone else was home. "It is almost time for dinner," thought Goldie. "I'm really glad to be a goldfish. I'm safe and sound and very well fed."

What does Tom look like? Draw a picture of Tom.

Drawing will vary.

Circle the picture that tells how Goldie feels.

Making Inferences

179

Mind-Reading Tricks

Samantha thought of a good joke. She bragged that she could read Maria's mind. She put her hand on Maria's head, closed her eyes, and said, "You had red punch with your lunch!"
"Wow! You're right!" replied Maria, not realizing that she had a little red ring around her lips.
"That was easy. But I bet you can't tell me what I just ate," said Thomas.
"That's a bunch of baloney," answered Samantha.
"How did you know?" gasped Thomas.
"It's my little secret," said Samantha, with a sigh of relief.
"Here comes your mom," said Maria. "Can you read her mind, too?"
Samantha looked down at her watch. She should have been home half an hour ago. As she ran to meet her mother, she yelled back, "Yes, I know exactly what she's thinking!"

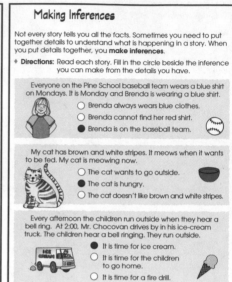

♦ **Directions:** Make inferences about Samantha's mind-reading tricks. Fill in the circle beside the correct inference.

1. Was Samantha sure that Thomas had eaten bologna for lunch?
   - ● No, she was just lucky
   - ○ Yes, she saw him eat his bologna sandwich.

2. What was Samantha's mother probably thinking?
   - ○ Samantha was a great mind reader.
   - ● Samantha was late.

Making Inferences

180

Answer Key

334

Tricky Cause and Effect

Things that happen can make other things happen. The event that happens is the **effect**. Why the event happens is the **cause**.

> **Example:** Marcie tripped on the step and fell down.
> **Cause:** Marcie tripped on the step.
> **Effect:** Marcie fell down.

♦ **Directions:** Read the story.

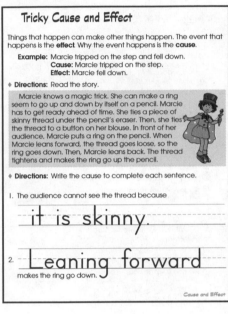

Marcie knows a magic trick. She can make a ring seem to go up and down by itself on a pencil. Marcie has to get ready ahead of time. She ties a piece of skinny thread under the pencil's eraser. Then, she ties the thread to a button on her blouse. In front of her audience, Marcie puts a ring on the pencil. When Marcie leans forward, the thread goes loose, so the ring goes down. Then, Marcie leans back. The thread tightens and makes the ring go up the pencil.

♦ **Directions:** Write the cause to complete each sentence.

1. The audience cannot see the thread because

it is skinny.

2. **Leaning forward**

makes the ring go down.

Cause and Effect

181

Why Did It Happen?

♦ **Directions:** Read the effects. Fill in the circle beside the sentence that tells what caused the effect.

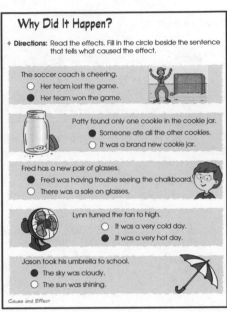

The soccer coach is cheering.
- ○ Her team lost the game.
- ● Her team won the game.

Patty found only one cookie in the cookie jar.
- ● Someone ate all the other cookies.
- ○ It was a brand new cookie jar.

Fred has a new pair of glasses.
- ● Fred was having trouble seeing the chalkboard.
- ○ There was a sale on glasses.

Lynn turned the fan to high.
- ○ It was a very cold day.
- ● It was a very hot day.

Jason took his umbrella to school.
- ● The sky was cloudy.
- ○ The sun was shining.

Cause and Effect

182

Chain of Effects

♦ **Directions:** Read the story.

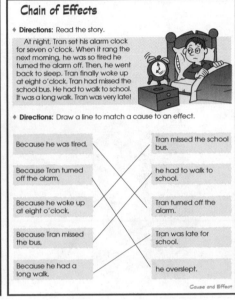

At night, Tran set his alarm clock for seven o'clock. When it rang the next morning, he was so tired he turned the alarm off. Then, he went back to sleep. Tran finally woke up at eight o'clock. Tran had missed the school bus. He had to walk to school. It was a long walk. Tran was very late!

♦ **Directions:** Draw a line to match a cause to an effect.

Because he was tired,	Tran missed the school bus.
Because Tran turned off the alarm,	he had to walk to school.
Because he woke up at eight o'clock,	Tran turned off the alarm.
Because Tran missed the bus,	Tran was late for school.
Because he had a long walk,	he overslept.

Cause and Effect

183

A Cause and Effect Fable

♦ **Directions:** Read the story.

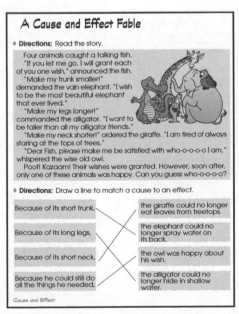

Four animals caught a talking fish. "If you let me go, I will grant each of you one wish," announced the fish. "Make my trunk smaller!" demanded the vain elephant. "I wish to be the most beautiful elephant that ever lived." "Make my legs longer!" commanded the alligator. "I want to be taller than all my alligator friends." "Make my neck shorter!" ordered the giraffe. "I am tired of always staring at the tops of trees." "Dear Fish, please make me satisfied with who-o-o-o-o I am," whispered the wise old owl. Poof! Kazaam! Their wishes were granted. However, soon after, only one of these animals was happy. Can you guess who-o-o-o-o?

♦ **Directions:** Draw a line to match a cause to an effect.

Because of its short trunk,	the giraffe could no longer eat leaves from treetops.
Because of its long legs,	the elephant could no longer spray water on its back.
Because of its short neck,	the owl was happy about his wish.
Because he could still do all the things he needed,	the alligator could no longer hide in shallow water.

Cause and Effect

184

What Comes Next?

It's fun to try to guess what will happen next as you read. Guessing what will happen is called **predicting outcomes**.

What you read: Liz drops the glass vase.

What you can predict: The glass vase will break.

♦ **Directions:** Read the story. Then, follow the directions below.

Every Saturday, Grace cleans her room. One Saturday, Grace forgot to clean it because she was busy playing with her cat, Tiger. Mom looked in and saw that Grace's room was still messy.

1. Complete the sentence to make a prediction.

Now, Grace will probably **get busy**

and clean her room.

2. Color the things Grace will probably hang in her closet.

Predicting Outcomes

185

What Will They Do?

♦ **Directions:** Read each sentence. Fill in the circle beside the best prediction. Then, circle the picture that matches your answer.

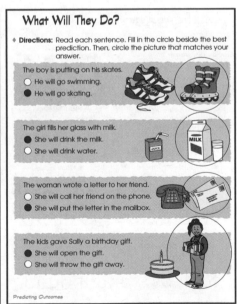

The boy is putting on his skates.
- ○ He will go swimming.
- ● He will go skating.

The girl fills her glass with milk.
- ● She will drink the milk.
- ○ She will drink water.

The woman wrote a letter to her friend.
- ○ She will call her friend on the phone.
- ● She will put the letter in the mailbox.

The kids gave Sally a birthday gift.
- ● She will open the gift.
- ○ She will throw the gift away.

Predicting Outcomes

186

335

Answer Key

Pup Predictions

♦ **Directions:** Read the story.

When Donald tells Dudley to sit, Dudley rolls over. If Donald asks him to come, Dudley runs away. To surprise Dad, Donald tries to teach Dudley to fetch the newspaper. Dudley rips it up! Donald will take Dudley to dog obedience school.

♦ **Directions:** Make predictions. Draw three things Dudley will probably learn in obedience school.

Drawings will show:
Dudley sitting.
Dudley fetching the newspaper.
Dudley coming to Donald when called.

Predicting Outcomes

187

How Will It End?

♦ **Directions:** Read each story. Fill in the circle beside the sentence that tells what will happen next.

It is a snowy winter night. The lights flicker once, twice, and then they go out. It is cold and dark. Dad finds the flashlight and matches. He brings logs in from outside. What will Dad do?

● Dad will make a fire.
○ Dad will cook dinner.
○ Dad will clean the fireplace.

Maggie has a garden. She likes fresh, homegrown vegetables. She says they make salads taste better. Maggie is going to make a salad for a picnic. What will Maggie do?

○ Maggie will buy the salad at the store.
○ Maggie will buy the vegetables at the store.
● Maggie will use vegetables from her garden.

The big white goose wakes up. It stands and stretches its wings. It looks all around. It feels very hungry. What will the goose do?

○ The goose will go swimming.
● The goose will look for food.
○ The goose will go back to sleep.

Predicting Outcomes

188

You Be the Judge

Story characters often have to make choices. As the reader, you decide whether or not the choices are good ones. This is called **making judgments**.

♦ **Directions:** Read the story.

On his way home from the park, Jason finds a baseball mitt under a bush. Alan tells Jason to keep the mitt because he is the one who found it. Arnold tells him to leave it there. Austin tells Jason to take it to the Lost and Found Department at the park. Jason looks inside the mitt. He can see a name and a telephone number.

Alan   Austin   Jason   Arnold

♦ **Directions:** Answer the questions.

Answers will vary but may include:

1. Who do you think gave the best advice? Austin

2. What do you think Jason should do? Jason should take the mitt to Lost and Found.

Making Judgments

191

Right or Wrong

♦ **Directions:** Read the story.

Today is Karl's day to have the ball at lunch recess. Danny forgets it is Karl's turn and takes the ball outside. Karl asks Danny for the ball. Danny won't give it to him. Karl grabs the ball from Danny and runs away from him.

♦ **Directions:** Make judgments about what each boy did wrong. Write a new ending for the story. Show how the boys could solve their problem without fighting.

Today is Karl's day to have the ball at lunch recess. Danny forgets it is Karl's turn and takes the ball outside. Karl asks Danny for the ball.

Sample answer:

Danny says he is sorry. He tells Karl he forgot it was not his turn. He gives Karl the ball.

Making Judgments

192

Judge for Yourself

♦ **Directions:** Read the story.

Arnold the Bully is trying to make friends. He isn't sure what he should do because he has always been a bully. He tries to buy friends by giving away his lunch and his toys. He listens to kids and doesn't boss them around. He takes turns and doesn't call names. He brags about what his dad does at work.

♦ **Directions:** Read each of Arnold's choices. Fill in the circle to show whether you think the choice is good or bad.

1. Arnold tries to buy friends.   ○ Good   ● Bad
2. Arnold listens to what kids say.   ● Good   ○ Bad
3. Arnold doesn't boss kids around.   ● Good   ○ Bad
4. Arnold takes turns.   ● Good   ○ Bad
5. Arnold doesn't call names.   ● Good   ○ Bad
6. Arnold brags about his dad.   ○ Good   ● Bad

Making Judgments

193

Answer Key

336

Which Brand Is the Best?

♦ **Directions:** Read the story.

Randy takes Pixie to the store to buy a big bag of dog food. All the dog food makers say their dog food is the best. The makers of Good Stuff say their food will give dogs longer lives. Best Ever dog food says it gives the extra vitamins dogs need for strong bones and teeth. Bits and Bits says it will give dogs good health and no bad dog breath.

♦ **Directions:** Fill in the circle beside the name of each person who would probably give Randy good advice about choosing a dog food.

● vet

○ cat lover

○ clerk selling Bits and Bits

● dog breeder

Making Judgments

194

Realistic Story or Fantasy?

Many stories are made-up stories. A made-up story about things that could really happen is a **realistic story**. Some made-up stories, such as fairy tales, tell about things that could never really happen. Those stories are **fantasies**.

Realistic Story: A girl hits a home run and wins the game for her team.

Fantasy: A girl hits the ball. It sprouts wings and flies away on an adventure.

♦ **Directions:** Read the book reviews. Fill in the circle to show whether each story is a realistic story or a fantasy.

The Flying Hippo is about a hippo that flies through the sky. He lands at a busy airport and wanders through New York City.
○ Realistic story   ● Fantasy

A Goose Learns to Fly is about a family who saves an injured baby goose. Later, they teach it to fly on its own.
● Realistic story   ○ Fantasy

The First Airplane is about the Wright Brothers and the airplane they invented.
● Realistic story   ○ Fantasy

The Magic Airplane is about a toy airplane that flies to the planet Mars.
○ Realistic story   ● Fantasy

Realism or Fantasy?

195

Fantasy Tales

If even one thing in a story could not really happen, the whole story is a fantasy.

♦ **Directions:** Read the stories. Underline the sentence that makes each story a fantasy.

Michelle got a kitten for her birthday. It was soft and cuddly. It liked to chase fuzzy toys. After playing, it napped in Michelle's lap. <u>One day the kitten said to Michelle, "Would you like me to tell you a story?"</u>

The team lined up. The kicker kicked the football. Up, up it soared. <u>It went up so high that it went into orbit around the Earth.</u> The game was over. The Aardvarks had won.

"This is a great car," the salesperson said. "It can go very fast. <u>It can cook your breakfast.</u> It always starts, even on the coldest day. You really should buy this car."

Chris studied about healthy food in school. He learned that milk could make him grow. Chris drank a glass of milk just before he went to bed. <u>When he got up in the morning, he was so tall, his head went right through the ceiling.</u>

Realism or Fantasy?

196

Write About Reality

♦ **Directions:** Write a journal entry. Write about a special day. You can make up the story, but make sure everything you write is something that could really happen.

Sample answer:

Yesterday our class went on a field trip. We rode a school bus to the zoo. We saw lions, bears and elephants. My favorite animals were the chimpanzees. They made faces at us. They did funny tricks, too. We had fun at the zoo.

Realism or Fantasy?

197

Write a Fantasy

♦ **Directions:** Write a new journal entry. Write about the same special day you

Sample answer:

Yesterday our class went on a field trip. We rode a school bus to the zoo. In the afternoon, it got very hot. I took off my hat and my jacket. Then I watched the chimpanzees. One chimp seemed to be looking at me. It did everything I did. I must have left my hat and jacket by the chimp's cage. The next thing I knew, the chimp was wearing my clothes. Nobody noticed when he climbed onto the school bus behind me. Now he is a regular member of the class. He is the class clown.

Realism or Fantasy?

198

Know Your Characters

Characters are the people or animals in a story. Understanding characters in a story helps you understand what happens. As you read, think about how you would act if you were the character. Think about how you would feel.

♦ **Directions:** Look at the pictures. Write words from the box to name the character's feelings.

glad   unhappy   pleased
sorry   sad   happy

unhappy   glad

sorry   pleased

sad   happy

Appreciating Literature

199

 337

Answer Key

Characters' Feelings

♦ **Directions:** Read the first sentence. Use a word from the box to complete the second sentence. Draw the correct expression on the character's face.

surprised   sad   angry

Eric's best friend moves to a new town.

He feels **sad**

A big bully pulls Julia's hair.

She feels **angry**

On Saturday, Harry sees a magic show.

He feels **surprised**

Appreciating Literature

200

Emotion Search

♦ **Directions:** Check the happy words. Circle them in the word search. The words go **across** and **down**.

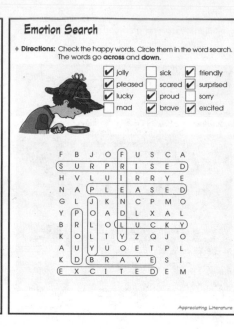

☑ jolly   ☐ sick   ☑ friendly
☑ pleased   ☐ scared   ☑ surprised
☑ lucky   ☑ proud   ☐ sorry
☐ mad   ☑ brave   ☑ excited

```
F  B  J  O  F  U  S  C  A
S  U  R  P  R  I  S  E  D
H  V  L  U  I  R  R  Y  E
N  A  P  L  E  A  S  E  D
G  L  J  K  N  C  P  M  O
Y  P  O  A  D  L  X  A  L
B  R  L  O  L  U  C  K  Y
K  O  Y  T  Y  Z  Q  J  O
A  U  D  U  O  E  T  P  L
K  D  B  R  A  V  E  S  I
E  X  C  I  T  E  D  E  M
```

Appreciating Literature

201

Getting to Know You

♦ **Directions:** Read the story.

Yesterday, my friend Rex and I visited the museum. We were excited about seeing the new dinosaur display.

"Wow!" I yelled when I looked up at the tyrannosaurus skeleton.

"He's my distant cousin," Rex joked. "In fact, I was named after him!"

"My cousin was really a picky eater," giggled Rex. "He's no skin, just bones!"

That night, I dreamed of that tyrannosaurus. I imagined him sticking his head into my bedroom window. I was too frightened to scream. When he opened his huge mouth, I froze.

"Do you know what happened to me because I wouldn't take a bath?" thundered the dinosaur.

I shook my head.

"I became x-stinked!" he roared.

Now, I think that Rex and his dinosaur "cousin" must really be related. They both tell bad jokes!

♦ **Directions:** Both Rex and his "cousin" like telling jokes. Circle the five words below that best describe the "cousins."

sad   (silly)   (funny)

(jolly)   brave

(comical)   (pranksters)

Appreciating Literature

202

Plot and Setting

Stories have a setting and a plot. The **setting** tells where and when the story takes place. The **plot** tells what happened.

♦ **Directions:** Read the story. Then, follow the directions below.

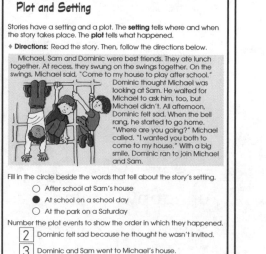

Michael, Sam and Dominic were best friends. They ate lunch together. At recess, they swung on the swings together. On the swings, Michael said, "Come to my house to play after school."

Dominic thought Michael was looking at Sam. He waited for Michael to ask him, too, but Michael didn't. All afternoon, Dominic felt sad. When the bell rang, he started to go home. "Where are you going?" Michael called. "I wanted you both to come to my house." With a big smile, Dominic ran to join Michael and Sam.

Fill in the circle beside the words that tell about the story's setting.

○ After school at Sam's house
● At school on a school day
○ At the park on a Saturday

Number the plot events to show the order in which they happened.

[2] Dominic felt sad because he thought he wasn't invited.

[3] Dominic and Sam went to Michael's house.

[1] Michael invited the boys over.

Appreciating Literature

203

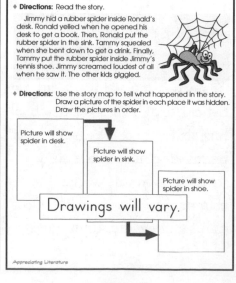

What's the Story?

♦ **Directions:** Read the story.

Jimmy hid a rubber spider inside Ronald's desk. Ronald yelled when he opened his desk to get a book. Then, Ronald put the rubber spider in the sink. Tammy squealed when she bent down to get a drink. Finally, Tammy put the rubber spider inside Jimmy's tennis shoe. Jimmy screamed loudest of all when he saw it. The other kids giggled.

♦ **Directions:** Use the story map to tell what happened in the story. Draw a picture of the spider in each place it was hidden. Draw the pictures in order.

Picture will show spider in desk.

Picture will show spider in sink.

Picture will show spider in shoe.

Drawings will vary.

Appreciating Literature

204

Do It Yourself Setting

When   Where

◆ **Directions:** Cut out each phrase. Sort the phrases into two stacks. Make one stack for phrases that tell when. Make another stack for phrases that tell where. Choose a card from each stack. Write or tell a story that has the setting the cards show.

before dinner	at the park
in the kitchen	during lunch
out in space	on the road
in the morning	at the pet shop
at one o'clock	at four o'clock
at school	on a train
in winter	at the zoo
in summer	on the ice
beside a ship	during breakfast
late at night	on a snow-covered mountain

Appreciating Literature

205

Critical Thinking

◆ **Directions:** Use your reading skills to answer each riddle. Unscramble the word to check your answer. Write the correct word on the line.

I am a ruler, but I have two feet, not one.

I am a **king**
(ngik)

I am very bright, but that doesn't make me smart.

I am the **sun**
(uns)

You can turn me around, but I won't get dizzy.

I am a **key**
(eky)

I can rattle, but I am not a baby's toy.

I am a **snake**
(nekas)

I will give you milk, but not in a bottle.

I am a **cow**
(ocw)

I smell, but I have no nose.

I am a **flower**
(oerflw)

Critical Thinking

207

Clues About Cats

◆ **Directions:** Read the clues carefully. Then, number the cats. When you are sure you are correct, color the cats.

1. A gray cat sits on the gate.
2. A cat with orange and black spots sits near the tree.
3. A brown cat sits near the bush.
4. A white cat sits between the orange and black spotted cat and the gray cat.
5. A black cat sits next to the brown cat.
6. An orange cat sits between the gray cat and the black cat.

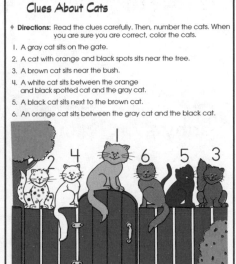

Critical Thinking

208

Hidden Meanings

◆ **Directions:** Cut out the cards. Use your thinking skills to match the picture words with their meanings.

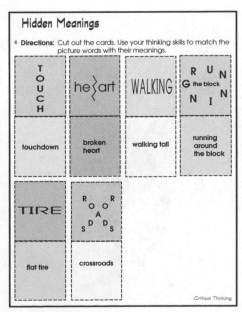

Critical Thinking

209

GRAMMAR AND WRITING

ABC Dots

◆ **Directions:** Connect the dots. Begin with **A**. Follow the letters of the alphabet.

Alphabetical Order

214

Answer Key

What Comes First?

The first letter of each word is used to put words in alphabetical (ABC) order.

Example: apple   bee   car

♦ **Directions:** Underline the first letter of each word. Then, write the words in alphabetical order.

sun   baby
1. baby
2. sun

nest   hen
1. hen
2. nest

jar   dog
1. dog
2. jar

girl   key
1. girl
2. key

Alphabetical Order

215

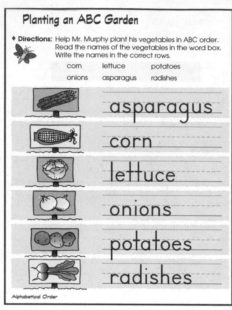

Planting an ABC Garden

♦ **Directions:** Help Mr. Murphy plant his vegetables in ABC order. Read the names of the vegetables in the word box. Write the names in the correct rows.

corn   lettuce   potatoes
onions   asparagus   radishes

asparagus
corn
lettuce
onions
potatoes
radishes

Alphabetical Order

216

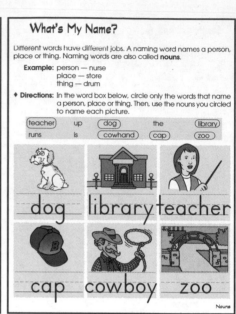

What's My Name?

Different words have different jobs. A naming word names a person, place or thing. Naming words are also called **nouns**.

Example: person — nurse
place — store
thing — drum

♦ **Directions:** In the word box below, circle only the words that name a person, place or thing. Then, use the nouns you circled to name each picture.

teacher   up   (dog)   the   (library)
runs   is   (cowhand)   (cap)   (zoo)

dog   library   teacher
cap   cowboy   zoo

Nouns

217

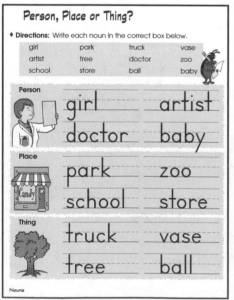

Person, Place or Thing?

♦ **Directions:** Write each noun in the correct box below.

girl   park   truck   vase
artist   tree   doctor   zoo
school   store   ball   baby

Person
girl   artist
doctor   baby

Place
park   zoo
school   store

Thing
truck   vase
tree   ball

Nouns

218

Finding Nouns

A noun names a person, place or thing.

♦ **Directions:** Circle two nouns in each sentence below.

The (pig) has a curly (tail).

The (hen) is sitting on her (nest).

A (horse) is in the (barn).

The (goat) has (horns).

The (cow) has a (calf).

The (farmer) is painting the (fence).

Nouns

219

Nouns at Play

♦ **Directions:** Complete each sentence with the correct noun from the word box. Write the noun on the line.

ducks	boys
dog	tree
sun	bird

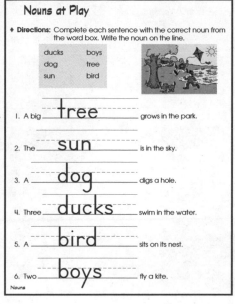

1. A big __tree__ grows in the park.

2. The __sun__ is in the sky.

3. A __dog__ digs a hole.

4. Three __ducks__ swim in the water.

5. A __bird__ sits on its nest.

6. Two __boys__ fly a kite.

Nouns

220

Proper Nouns

Some nouns are special. They name particular persons, places and things. They are called **proper nouns**. Proper nouns always begin with capital letters.

Example: person — Gina
place — Main Street
thing — Golden Gate Bridge

♦ **Directions:** Fill in the circle beside the sentence that is written correctly.

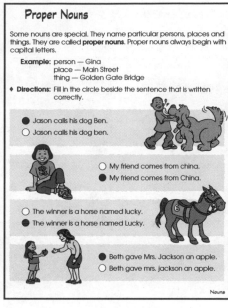

● Jason calls his dog Ben.
○ Jason calls his dog ben.

○ My friend comes from china.
● My friend comes from China.

○ The winner is a horse named lucky.
● The winner is a horse named Lucky.

● Beth gave Mrs. Jackson an apple.
○ Beth gave mrs. jackson an apple.

Nouns

221

One or More Than One?

♦ **Directions:** Circle the correct word under each picture.

hat (hats)   car cars   frog (frogs)

(shirt) shirts   cloud (clouds)   wheel (wheels)

dish (dishes)   glass (glasses)   (fox) foxes

Nouns

222

How Many Toys?

♦ **Directions:** Read the nouns under the pictures. Write each noun under **One** or **More Than One**.

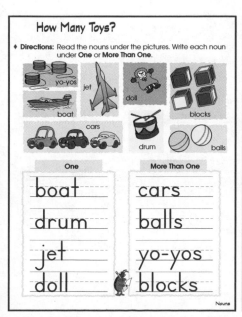

yo-yos   jet   doll   blocks
boat   cars   drum   balls

One	More Than One
boat	cars
drum	balls
jet	yo-yos
doll	blocks

Nouns

223

Making Nouns Plural

A **plural noun** means more than one. Add **s** to most nouns to make plural nouns.

Example: Penny has one **dog**.
Jerry has two **dogs**.

♦ **Directions:** Write the plural form of the nouns below.

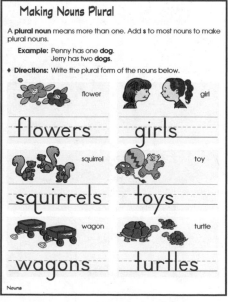

flower — __flowers__   girl — __girls__

squirrel — __squirrels__   toy — __toys__

wagon — __wagons__   turtle — __turtles__

Nouns

224

One Is Not Enough!

A plural noun means more than one. To make nouns that end in **x, s, ss, sh** or **ch** plural, add **es**.

Example: Barry filled one **box** with sand.
Barry filled four **boxes** with sand.

♦ **Directions:** Write the plural form of each noun below.

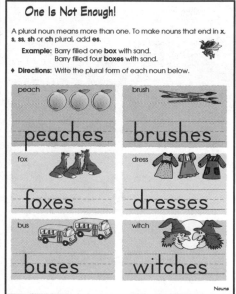

peach — __peaches__   brush — __brushes__

fox — __foxes__   dress — __dresses__

bus — __buses__   witch — __witches__

Nouns

225

Answer Key

Use the Clues

♦ **Directions:** Write each word from the word box in the correct place. Remember that plural forms usually end in **s.**

kites   star   chick   foxes   matches   lunch

One

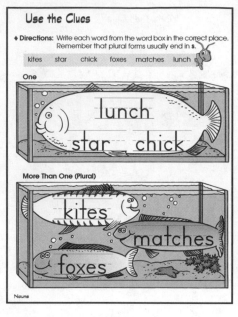

lunch
star   chick

More Than One (Plural)

kites
matches
foxes

Nouns

226

Ready, Set, Go!

An **action word** tells what a person or thing can do.

Example: Fred **kicks** the ball.

♦ **Directions:** Read the words below. Circle words that tell what the children are doing.

jump
boy

sleep
bed

hello
talk

skate
mittens

hop
sidewalk

sing
song

swim
deep

story
read

Verbs

227

Action Words

♦ **Directions:** Underline the action word in each sentence. Then, draw a line to match each sentence with the correct picture.

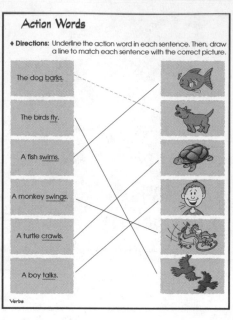

The dog barks.

The birds fly.

A fish swims.

A monkey swings.

A turtle crawls.

A boy talks.

Verbs

228

What Is a Verb?

A **verb** is an action word. A verb tells what a person or thing does.

Example: Jane **reads** a book.

♦ **Directions:** Circle the verb in each sentence below.

Two tiny dogs dance

The bear climbs a ladder.

The clown falls down.

A tiger jumps through a ring.

A boy eats popcorn.

A woman swings on a trapeze.

Verbs

229

Verbs With One

Some verbs tell what one person or thing does. Most of those verbs end in **s.**

Example: Boys **like** pets.
One boy **likes** pets.

♦ **Directions:** Add **s** to each verb to make it tell about one. Write the verb.

Many fish swim. One fish   swims

Snakes glide. One snake   glides

Rabbits hop. One rabbit   hops

Dogs bark. One dog   barks

Birds sing. One bird   sings

Verbs

230

Using Is, Are and Am

The words **is, are** and **am** are special verbs.

Use **is** to tell about one person or thing.
Use **are** to tell about more than one.

Use **are** with the word **you.** Use **am** with the word **I.**

♦ **Directions:** Write **is, are** or **am** in each sentence below.

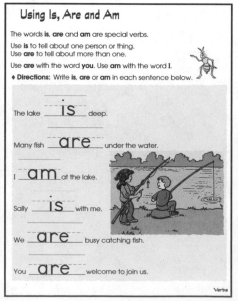

The lake   is   deep.

Many fish   are   under the water.

I   am   at the lake.

Sally   is   with me.

We   are   busy catching fish.

You   are   welcome to join us.

Verbs

231

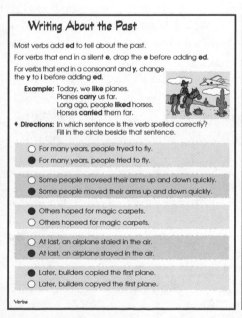

Now or in the Past

A verb can tell about something that happened in the past. For most verbs, add **ed** to tell about the past.

Example: Today, Tara and Jim **walk** to school.
Yesterday, Tara and Jim **walked** to school.

♦ Directions: Write the correct verb in each sentence.

follow, followed
Two weeks ago, a puppy **followed** me home.

seems, seemed
The puppy **seemed** hungry.

look, looked
Last week, we **looked** for its owner.

play, played
Now, the puppy and I **play** every day.

waits, waited
She **waits** at home for me when I am at school.

Verbs

232

Doubling Final Consonants

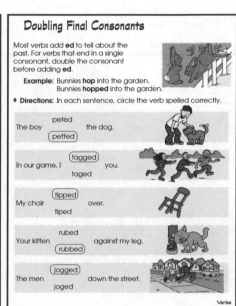

Most verbs add **ed** to tell about the past. For verbs that end in a single consonant, double the consonant before adding **ed**.

Example: Bunnies **hop** into the garden.
Bunnies **hopped** into the garden.

♦ Directions: In each sentence, circle the verb spelled correctly.

The boy peted / (petted) the dog.

In our game, I (tagged) / taged you.

My chair (tipped) / tiped over.

Your kitten rubed / (rubbed) against my leg.

The men (jogged) / joged down the street.

Verbs

233

Writing About the Past

Most verbs add **ed** to tell about the past.

For verbs that end in a silent **e**, drop the **e** before adding **ed**.

For verbs that end in a consonant and **y**, change the **y** to **i** before adding **ed**.

Example: Today, we **like** planes.
Planes **carry** us far.
Long ago, people **liked** horses.
Horses **carried** them far.

♦ Directions: In which sentence is the verb spelled correctly? Fill in the circle beside that sentence.

- ○ For many years, people tryed to fly.
- ● For many years, people tried to fly.

- ○ Some people mooved their arms up and down quickly.
- ● Some people moved their arms up and down quickly.

- ● Others hoped for magic carpets.
- ○ Others hopeed for magic carpets.

- ○ At last, an airplane staied in the air.
- ● At last, an airplane stayed in the air.

- ● Later, builders copied the first plane.
- ○ Later, builders copyed the first plane.

Verbs

234

Verbs That Change

Some verbs change in special ways to tell about the past. Here are a few important verbs that change in special ways.

♦ Directions: In each sentence, write a verb from the box to tell about the past.

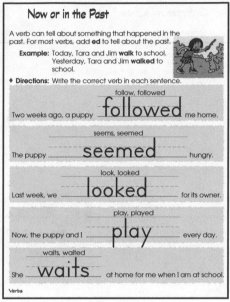

Now	Past	Now	Past
come	came	make	made
eat	ate	run	ran
have, has	had	write	wrote

My grandmother **wrote** me a letter.

At lunch yesterday, I **ate** an orange.

Last week, we **came** home from a trip.

This morning, we **ran** in a race.

Last winter, I **had** some blue gloves, but now I have red ones.

Verbs

235

Using Was and Were

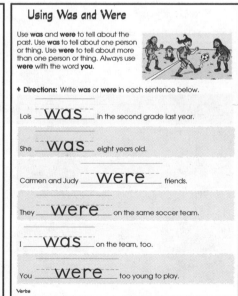

Use **was** and **were** to tell about the past. Use **was** to tell about one person or thing. Use **were** to tell about more than one person or thing. Always use **were** with the word **you**.

♦ Directions: Write **was** or **were** in each sentence below.

Lois **was** in the second grade last year.

She **was** eight years old.

Carmen and Judy **were** friends.

They **were** on the same soccer team.

I **was** on the team, too.

You **were** too young to play.

Verbs

236

Answer Key

Using the Verb Give

Use **give** and **gives** to tell about now.
Use **gave** to tell about the past.

♦ **Directions:** Write **give**, **gives** or **gave** in each sentence below.

Trisha _gave_ a party last week.

Bananas _give_ me a rash.

I _give_ my dog some water every day.

Jill _gave_ the jacket to me yesterday.

The teacher always _gives_ a test on Friday.

She _gave_ Mike a turn as line leader yesterday.

Verbs

237

Contraction Action

You can combine two words to make one new word. If you leave out a letter and add the mark ' in its place, you make a **contraction**. To make some contractions, combine a verb and the word **not**.

Example: is + not = isn̶o̶t = isn't

♦ **Directions:** Match these verbs and the word **not** with the contractions.

does + not — haven't
should + not — isn't
is + not — doesn't
have + not — shouldn't

♦ **Directions:** Choose the contraction for the underlined words. Fill in the circle beside the correct contraction.

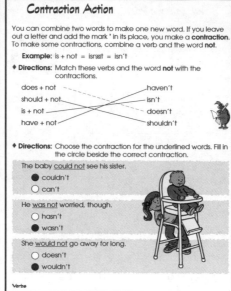

The baby <u>could not</u> see his sister.
● couldn't
○ can't

He <u>was not</u> worried, though.
○ hasn't
● wasn't

She <u>would not</u> go away for long.
○ doesn't
● wouldn't

Verbs

238

Words That Describe

Some words describe a person, place or thing. These words tell more about a naming word.

Example: The shoe is **old**.

♦ **Directions:** Read these words that describe. Write the correct word under each picture.

| cold | round | funny |
| light | sad | fat |

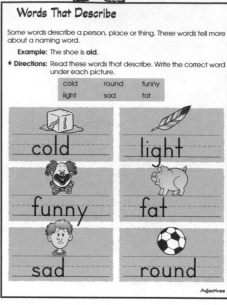

cold | light
funny | fat
sad | round

Adjectives

239

Describe It!

♦ **Directions:** Match the describing word with the correct picture.

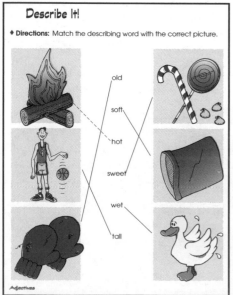

old
soft
hot
sweet
wet
tall

Adjectives

240

Tell Me More!

A **describing word** tells about a noun. It can tell what kind, what color, what size, what shape or how many.

♦ **Directions:** Write a describing word in each sentence below. Use the words in the box.

| green | big | three | round | bushy | six |

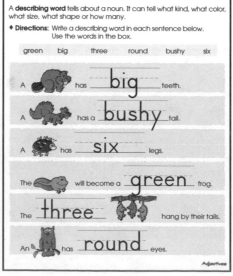

A _big_ has teeth.

A _bushy_ has a tail.

A _six_ has legs.

The _green_ will become a frog.

The _three_ hang by their tails.

An _round_ has eyes.

Adjectives

241

What Is It Like?

Describing words tell about persons, places and things. They can tell how things look, taste, sound or feel.

♦ **Directions:** Circle two describing words in each sentence below.

The (white) kitten is (fluffy.)

(Noisy) squirrels ran up a (tall) tree.

The (old) book is (torn.)

The apple was (sweet) and (crisp.)

The (bright) sun is (warm.)

(Yellow) ducks swam in a (little) pond.

Adjectives

242

Answer Key

344

© 2001 McGraw Hill Education. All Rights Reserved.

What Color Is It?

Color words are describing words.

Example: Sue has a **blue** dress.
The banana is **yellow**.

♦ **Directions:** Underline the color words in these sentences. Use these describing words to help you color the picture.

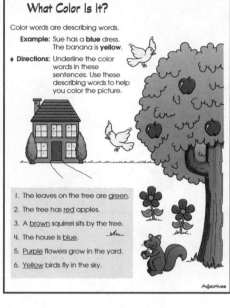

1. The leaves on the tree are <u>green</u>.
2. The tree has <u>red</u> apples.
3. A <u>brown</u> squirrel sits by the tree.
4. The house is <u>blue</u>.
5. <u>Purple</u> flowers grow in the yard.
6. <u>Yellow</u> birds fly in the sky.

Adjectives

243

Weather Words

Weather words are describing words. They tell what kind.

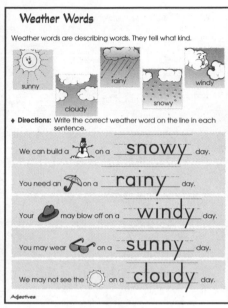

sunny
cloudy
rainy
snowy
windy

♦ **Directions:** Write the correct weather word on the line in each sentence.

We can build a ☃ on a __snowy__ day.

You need an ☂ on a __rainy__ day.

Your 🎩 may blow off on a __windy__ day.

You may wear 🕶 on a __sunny__ day.

We may not see the ☀ on a __cloudy__ day.

Adjectives

244

How Many Do You See?

Number words are describing words. They tell how many.

Example: **Two** ants crawled across the table.

♦ **Directions:** Read the sentences below. In each sentence, underline the describing word that tells how many. Then, look at the picture. Write an **X** after the sentence that uses an incorrect number word.

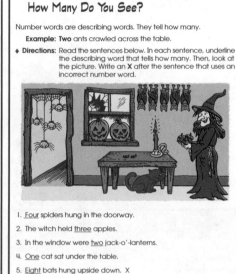

1. <u>Four</u> spiders hung in the doorway.
2. The witch held <u>three</u> apples.
3. In the window were <u>two</u> jack-o'-lanterns.
4. <u>One</u> cat sat under the table.
5. <u>Eight</u> bats hung upside down. X

245

Fish for Describing Words

♦ **Directions:** Color only the fish with describing words.

rug
sunny
loud
warm
quilt
green
moan
good
big
bed
old
hot

Adjectives

246

Telling the Whole Story

A **sentence** tells a whole idea.

♦ **Directions:** Read each sentence. Write the number by the correct picture. Color the pictures.

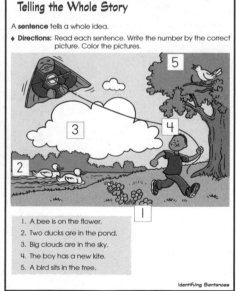

1. A bee is on the flower.
2. Two ducks are in the pond.
3. Big clouds are in the sky.
4. The boy has a new kite.
5. A bird sits in the tree.

Identifying Sentences

247

Answer Key

Choosing Sentences

A sentence must tell a whole idea.

♦ **Directions:** Read each group of words. Color the airplane red if the words make a sentence. Color the airplane blue if the words do not make a sentence.

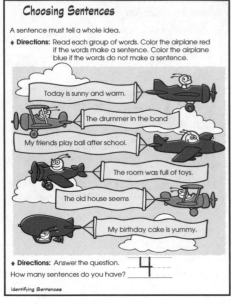

Today is sunny and warm.

The drummer in the band

My friends play ball after school.

The room was full of toys.

The old house seems

My birthday cake is yummy.

♦ **Directions:** Answer the question.
How many sentences do you have? ___4___

Identifying Sentences

248

Writing Sentences Right

A sentence always begins with a capital letter.

Example: The sun is shining.

♦ **Directions:** Write each sentence correctly.

the wind is strong.

The wind is strong.

we made a snowman.

We made a snowman.

puddles are fun.

Puddles are fun.

leaves fell all day.

Leaves fell all day.

Identifying Sentences

249

A Big Finish

Every sentence ends with one of these end marks.

. ? !

♦ **Directions:** Fill in the circle beside the sentence that is written correctly.

● Terry has new skates.
○ Terry has new skates

○ Watch her zoom
● Watch her zoom!

● Does she wear pads on her knees?
○ Does she wear pads on her knees

○ Wear a helmet when you skate.
● Wear a helmet when you skate.

● Skating is fun!
○ Skating is fun

Identifying Sentences

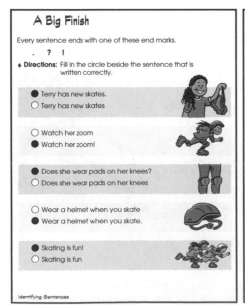

250

Sentence Building Blocks

Every sentence has two parts. The **naming part** tells who or what is doing something. The **action part**

♦ **Directions:** Match each naming part with an action part that makes sense.

Naming part	Action part
My sister	has wings.
That bird	likes ice cream.

tells what the person or thing does.

The little boy	cluck.
The goat	takes a picture.
The hens	eats grass.

Mom	walks by the cart.
Mike	rides in the cart.
Little Amy	pushes the cart.

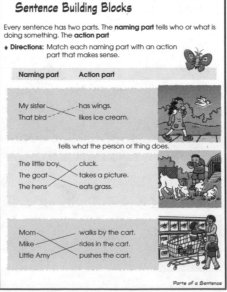

Parts of a Sentence

251

Completing Sentences

♦ **Directions:** Each sentence is missing either a naming part or an action part. Fill in the circle beside the group of words that forms the missing part.

My neighbor _____
● is having a yard sale today. ○ in the house next door.

One man _____
○ at the sale. ● likes old books.

_____ look for old toys.
● Many people ○ In the morning

_____ wants an old checkers game.
○ By the door ● My brother

Two ladies _____
● buy an old toy chest. ○ a teddy bear.

Parts of a Sentence

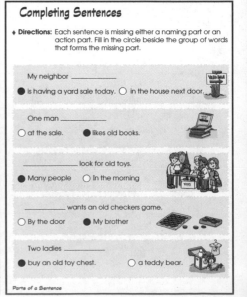

252

Finding Naming Parts

The naming part of a sentence tells who or what is doing something.

Example: The **chimp on a bike** rode in a circle.

♦ **Directions:** Underline the naming part in each sentence below.

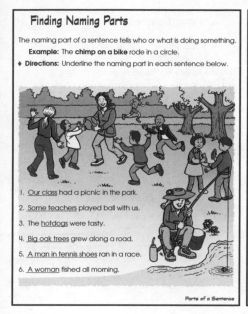

1. <u>Our class</u> had a picnic in the park.
2. <u>Some teachers</u> played ball with us.
3. The <u>hotdogs</u> were tasty.
4. <u>Big oak trees</u> grew along a road.
5. <u>A man in tennis shoes</u> ran in a race.
6. <u>A woman</u> fished all morning.

Parts of a Sentence

253

Writing Naming Parts

♦ **Directions:** Read the naming parts in the tent. Write one of the naming parts to begin each sentence.

Rain   Todd and Clint
Black clouds   The old tent
A big wind

1. Todd and Clint went camping.
2. The old tent was hard to set up.
3. A big wind blew the trees.
4. Black clouds filled the sky.
5. Rain fell on the tent.

Parts of a Sentence

254

Action at the Zoo

The action part of a sentence tells what the naming part is doing or did.

Example: The zookeeper **opened the gate**.

♦ **Directions:** Underline the action part in each sentence below.

1. My family <u>walked to the zoo</u>.
2. The seals <u>swam in a pool of water</u>.
3. A monkey <u>climbed a tree</u>.
4. Two big elephants <u>swung their trunks</u>.
5. A striped tiger <u>paced in its cage</u>.
6. The giraffe <u>stretched its long neck</u>.

Parts of a Sentence

255

It's Time for Action!

♦ **Directions:** Write one of these action parts to finish each sentence.

came from the roof
put out the fire
raced to the fire
blew loudly
held a big hose

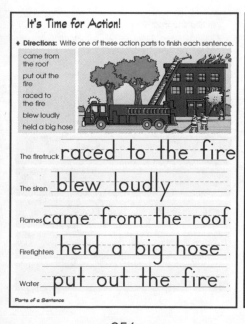

The firetruck raced to the fire
The siren blew loudly
Flames came from the roof
Firefighters held a big hose
Water put out the fire

Parts of a Sentence

256

Circus Sentences

♦ **Directions:** The boxes at the bottom of this page have sentence parts. Some are naming parts. Some are action parts. Cut out all the boxes. Look at each picture. Glue the correct naming part and action part beside each picture. Read each sentence that you make.

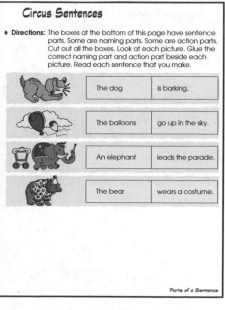

The dog	is barking.
The balloons	go up in the sky.
An elephant	leads the parade.
The bear	wears a costume.

Parts of a Sentence

257

Is Anything Missing?

♦ **Directions:** Read each group of words. Is it a complete sentence that tells a whole idea? Is it missing a naming part? Is it missing an action part? Fill in the circle beside the correct answer.

is going to the big game tonight
○ Complete sentence
● Missing a naming part
○ Missing an action part

The fans cheer for their team.
● Complete sentence
○ Missing a naming part
○ Missing an action part

Hot dogs
○ Complete sentence
○ Missing a naming part
● Missing an action part

The cheerleaders jump and yell for our team.
● Complete sentence
○ Missing a naming part
○ Missing an action part

Parts of a Sentence

259

Answer Key

Sentences That Tell

Some sentences tell something. Every **telling sentence** ends with a **period**.

Example: The bird sings.

♦ **Directions:** Circle only the sentences that tell something.

1. (Two turtles sat on a log.)
2. (One turtle fell off.)
3. Did you see her?
4. (She swam away.)
5. (The water is cold.)
6. Can you swim?

Kinds of Sentences

260

Sentences That Ask

Some sentences ask something. An **asking sentence** is called a **question**. A question ends with a **question mark**.

Example: What is your name?

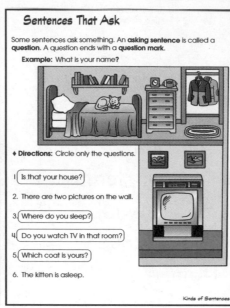

♦ **Directions:** Circle only the questions.

1. (Is that your house?)
2. There are two pictures on the wall.
3. (Where do you sleep?)
4. (Do you watch TV in that room?)
5. (Which coat is yours?)
6. The kitten is asleep.

Kinds of Sentences

261

Questions, Questions

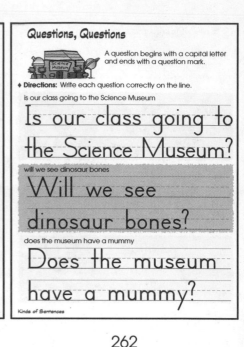

A question begins with a capital letter and ends with a question mark.

♦ **Directions:** Write each question correctly on the line.

is our class going to the Science Museum

Is our class going to the Science Museum?

will we see dinosaur bones

Will we see dinosaur bones?

does the museum have a mummy

Does the museum have a mummy?

Kinds of Sentences

262

Are You Telling or Asking?

A telling sentence ends with a period. A question ends with a question mark.

♦ **Directions:** Read each sentence. Put the correct end mark after each sentence.

1. Is winter coming [?]
2. Snow is falling in the woods [.]
3. The trees are covered with snow [.]
4. Is the bear lost [?]
5. The bear is looking for his cave [.]
6. The bear is cold and sleepy [.]
7. Is the bear ready for a long nap [?]
8. Will the bear sleep all winter [?]

Kinds of Sentences

263

Changing Sentences

The order of words can change a sentence.

Example: **Telling sentence:** The girl can jump high.
Asking sentence: Can the girl jump high?

♦ **Directions:** Read each telling sentence. Change the order of the words to make a question. Write your question on the line.

The clown is happy.

Is the clown happy?

The boy can swim.

Can the boy swim?

The bell will ring.

Will the bell ring?

The popcorn is hot.

Is the popcorn hot?

Kinds of Sentences

264

I'm So Excited!

The end mark ! shows that you are excited. Use it to end a sentence that shows strong feelings.

Example: What a beautiful day this is!

? or !

♦ **Directions:** Read these sentences. Write ? or ! after each sentence.

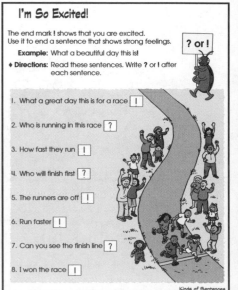

1. What a great day this is for a race [!]
2. Who is running in this race [?]
3. How fast they run [!]
4. Who will finish first [?]
5. The runners are off [!]
6. Run faster [!]
7. Can you see the finish line [?]
8. I won the race [!]

Kinds of Sentences

265

Follow My Directions.

You can write orders in sentences. If you are excited, end your order with !. If you are not excited, end your order with a period.

Example: Watch out for that hole in the road!
Ride slowly.

♦ **Directions:** Fill in the circle beside the sentence that is written correctly.

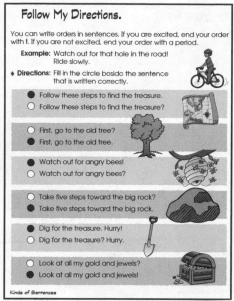

- ● Follow these steps to find the treasure.
- ○ Follow these steps to find the treasure?

- ○ First, go to the old tree?
- ● First, go to the old tree.

- ● Watch out for angry bees!
- ○ Watch out for angry bees?

- ○ Take five steps toward the big rock?
- ● Take five steps toward the big rock.

- ● Dig for the treasure. Hurry!
- ○ Dig for the treasure? Hurry.

- ○ Look at all my gold and jewels?
- ● Look at all my gold and jewels!

Kinds of Sentences

266

Sentence Combining

Two sentences can become one sentence. Use the word **and** to join them. Leave out words that are repeated.

Example: I have a ball. I have a bat.
I have a ball **and** a bat.

♦ **Directions:** Read the two sentences. Write them as one sentence.

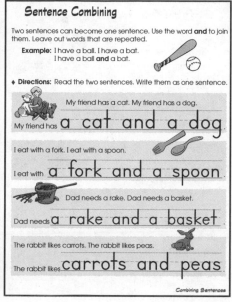

My friend has a cat. My friend has a dog.
My friend has a cat and a dog

I eat with a fork. I eat with a spoon.
I eat with a fork and a spoon

Dad needs a rake. Dad needs a basket.
Dad needs a rake and a basket

The rabbit likes carrots. The rabbit likes peas.
The rabbit likes carrots and peas

Combining Sentences

267

Using and in Sentences

Two sentences can become one sentence. You can use the word **and** to join them.

Examples: Maria sings. She hums, too.   Maria sings **and** hums.
Maria sings. Sean sings, too.   Maria **and** Sean sing.

♦ **Directions:** Read the two sentences. Write them as one sentence.

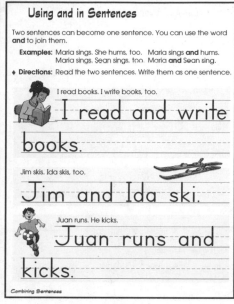

I read books. I write books, too.
I read and write books.

Jim skis. Ida skis, too.
Jim and Ida ski.

Juan runs. He kicks.
Juan runs and kicks.

Combining Sentences

268

Combining Sentences

♦ **Directions:** Read the two sentences. Find the sentence parts below that tell the same idea. Cut out and glue the sentence parts to make one sentence.

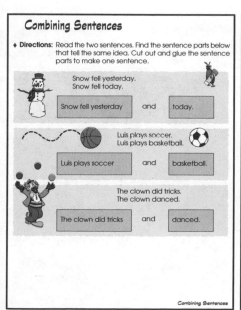

Snow fell yesterday.
Snow fell today.

| Snow fell yesterday | and | today. |

Luis plays soccer.
Luis plays basketball.

| Luis plays soccer | and | basketball. |

The clown did tricks.
The clown danced.

| The clown did tricks | and | danced. |

Combining Sentences

269

Pulling It All Together

♦ **Directions:** Read the two sentences. Write them as one sentence.

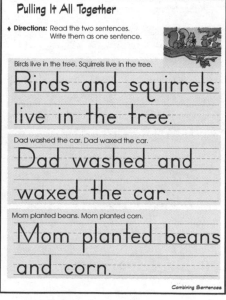

Birds live in the tree. Squirrels live in the tree.
Birds and squirrels live in the tree.

Dad washed the car. Dad waxed the car.
Dad washed and waxed the car.

Mom planted beans. Mom planted corn.
Mom planted beans and corn.

Combining Sentences

271

One Word at a Time

A sentence makes sense when the words are in order.

♦ **Directions:** Write the numerals 1, 2, 3 and 4 in the circles to put the words in order. Write the words in the correct order to make a sentence.

④ painting. ② doghouse ③ needs ① The

The doghouse needs painting.

② have ① I ④ paint. ③ red

I have red paint.

④ happy. ③ very ② is ① Spot

Spot is very happy.

Building Sentences

272

349

Answer Key

Groups of Words

Changing groups of words in a sentence changes the meaning.

Example: The boy is **in the car**.

The boy is **in the water**.

♦ **Directions:** Cut out and glue a word group to complete each sentence. Draw a picture to show the meaning of the sentence. Color the picture.

Answers may vary.

1. The fish | in the bowl | is yellow.

Drawings will vary.

2. I see a kite | with a smiley face |

3. That box | of oranges | is yours.

Building Sentences

273

Word Order

Changing the order of the words in a sentence may change the meaning.

Example: The dog chased the cat.

The cat chased the dog.

♦ **Directions:** Read the sentence pairs. Circle the sentence that goes with the picture.

(The boy hit the ball.)
The ball hit the boy.

The giant watched the elf.
(The elf watched the giant.)

The teacher read to the girl.
(The girl read to the teacher.)

(The baby laughed at the father.)
The father laughed at the baby.

The frog jumped over the rabbit.
(The rabbit jumped over the frog.)

Building Sentences

275

What Kind?

Words that describe make a sentence better.

Example: I have a coat.
I have a **red** coat **with many pockets**.

♦ **Directions:** Read each sentence. Write a word from the box on each line to make the sentences more interesting. Draw a picture of each sentence.

| bright | strong | little |
| brave | graceful | precious |

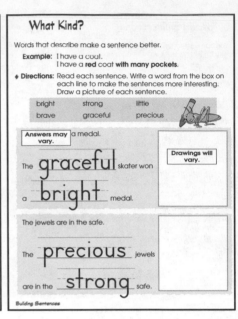

Answers may vary. a medal.

The **graceful** skater won a **bright** medal.

Drawings will vary.

The jewels are in the safe.

The **precious** jewels are in the **strong** safe.

Building Sentences

276

How Does It Happen?

A sentence can tell what a person or thing does. It can also tell how, when or where the person or thing does the action.

Example: Ada walked.
Then, Ada walked quickly from the room.

How? quickly **When?** Then **Where?** from the room

♦ **Directions:** In each sentence, write a word or words to answer the question. If you like, use words from this box.

| noisily | in the show | at night | before lunch | on the stage |
| loudly | around | nearby | in the yard | with energy |

Answers may vary.

My dog was barking **loudly** . How?

My dog was barking **at night** . When?

Dave sang **in the show** . Where?

The girls play **nearby** . Where?

They play **with energy** . How?

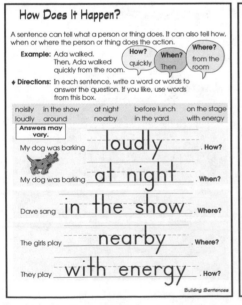

Building Sentences

277

A Sentence That Grows

A sentence can tell more and more.

♦ **Directions:** Make the underlined sentence grow by writing a word on each line. On another paper, draw a picture of the last sentence.

I see the elephant.

Sample answers:

I see the **hungry** elephant.

I see the **hungry** elephant eating **peanuts**

I see the **hungry** elephant eating **peanuts** as he stands by the **fence**

Building Sentences

278

Another Growing Sentence

♦ **Directions:** Complete the first sentence. Make it grow by writing a word on each line. On another sheet of paper, draw a picture of the last sentence.

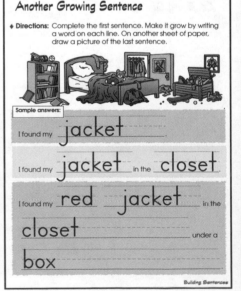

Sample answers:

I found my **jacket**

I found my **jacket** in the **closet**

I found my **red jacket** in the **closet** under a **box**

Building Sentences

279

Answer Key

350

Joining Sentences

You can join sentences to tell more.

Example: Linda went to the store, **and** I met her there.

Linda went to the store, **but** she didn't buy anything.

◆ **Directions:** What can you join to the sentence to make it tell more? Fill in the circle beside the right ending.

It snowed yesterday, and
- ● my friends and I made a snowman.
- ○ flowers are pretty.

Jerry had a party, but
- ○ some people skate well.
- ● not everyone could come.

This book is long, but
- ○ carrots are good for you.
- ● it is not hard.

The baseball game was called off, and
- ○ we like to swim.
- ● I went home.

Building Sentences

280

More on Joining Sentences

You can join sentences to tell more about something.

Example: Julian read a book.
Julian read a book **when** he got home.

◆ **Directions:** Read each sentence. Cut and glue to make the joined sentences tell more.

Tom likes to go to the library.

Tom likes to go to the library | when he has free time.

Pete did not do his homework.

Pete did not do his homework | because he was sick.

Will you call me?

Will you call me | as soon as you can?

Tina is saving her money.

Tina is saving her money | because she wants a bike.

Building Sentences

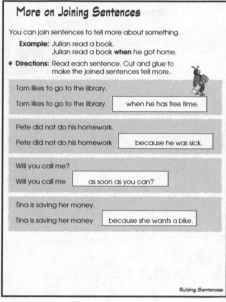

281

Adding Why

You can make sentences that tell more. You can add why something happened.

◆ **Directions:** Read the beginning of each sentence. Complete each sentence by telling why something happened.

There was no school yesterday **because**

Jerry had a party **because**

Answers will vary.

I am leaving now **because**

Building Sentences

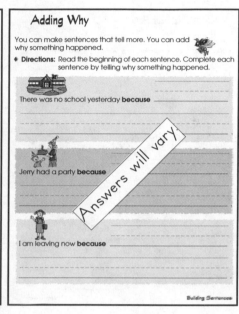

283

Telling a Story in Order

Tell the events of a story in the order they happened. Use the words **first**, **next** and **last** to make the order clear.

◆ **Directions:** The three pictures tell a story. The sentences should tell the same story. Read the given sentence. Then, write two sentences to complete the story.

Sample answers:

First: Kim found a bird that was hurt.

Next: Kim took the bird to a vet who helped it.

Last: The bird flew away.

Order of Events

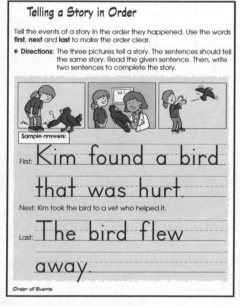

284

What Happened Next?

Sentences can tell about events in the order they happened.

◆ **Directions:** Read the sentence. Write two sentences to tell what two things could happen next. Draw a picture to match an event in your story.

Sample answer: e shelter to choose a new pet.

The dog wagged its tail and begged. Sally chose the dog as her new pet.

Drawings will vary.

Order of Events

285

Using Sentences in Order

Sentences can tell events in a story in order.

◆ **Directions:** Write 1, 2 and 3 in the circles to tell what happened to Harry first, second and third. Then, write a sentence to tell about each picture. You can use the words from the box in your sentences if you need them.

boat
catch
caught
fight
fish
fought
pole
proud

Answers will vary.

Order of Events

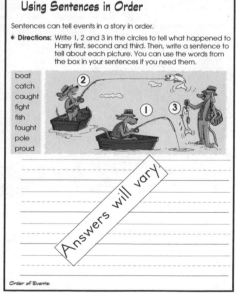

286

351

Answer Key

What Did You Say?

A sentence can tell what someone is saying.

♦ **Directions:** Look at each picture. Write a sentence in the bubble that tells what the person is saying.

Answers will vary.

Writing Sentences

287

Writing a Letter

Sentences can make a good letter.

♦ **Directions:** Write a letter to a friend on the lines.

Dear _____

Answers will vary.

Your friend,

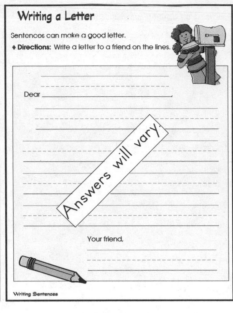

Writing Sentences

288

Writing About the Seasons

Sentences can tell about special times. Every season of the year is special.

♦ **Directions:** Write three words to tell about each season.

Spring

Summer

Answers will vary.

Fall

Winter

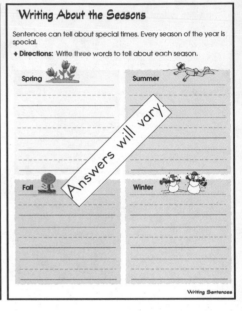

Writing Sentences

289

Let's Take a Trip!

Sentences can tell about special happenings.

♦ **Directions:** Imagine you are going somewhere far away. On the short lines in and around the plane, write words about your trip. Then, use some of the words to write three sentences about the trip.

Answers will vary.

Writing Sentences

290

Brainstorming

Brainstorming is a way to think of new ideas. You can use these ideas in your writing.

♦ **Directions:** Answer the questions below. Use the answers to help you write four sentences about your family.

My Family

How many people are in your family? _____

What are their names? _____

Answers will vary.

Write two words that tell _____ person.

What is your family's favorite meal? _____

What is your family's favorite TV show? _____

Writing Sentences

291

All About Me

♦ **Directions:** Write sentences to tell about yourself.

Draw yourself.

Drawings will vary.

Answers will vary.

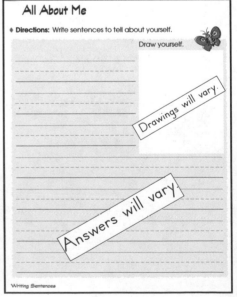

Writing Sentences

292

Answer Key

352